GRANT WRITING
For Teachers and Administrators

Grant Writing For Teachers and Administrators

by Bruce Sliger

Strategic Book Publishing
New York, NewYork

Strategic Book Publishing
An imprint of AEG Publishing Group
845 Third Avenue, 6th Floor - 6016
New York, NY 10022
www.StrategicBookPublishing.com

ISBN: 978-1-60860-131-8
SKU: 1-60860-131-5

Printed in the United States of America

Book Design: Rolando F. Santos

Contents

Figures and Tables

Dedication

This book is dedicated to my parents, my wife, my sons,
and all those educators who go that extra mile for their students.

Acknowledgements

Adell Atwood, Julie Coleman, Glenda Davis, Dr. Mack Duggins, Dr. Penny Elkins, Charlene Fowler, Robert Frady, Dr. Allison Gilmore, Jeffery Jackson, Sharon Johnson, Dr. Carl Martray, Terry Menard, Karen Miller, Eliot Rosenberg, Dr. Peter Ross, Melissa Sutton, Ashley Williams

Introduction

Grant Writing for Educators

A FEW years ago, I was appointed principal of a brand-new elementary school. The faculty and I began sorting out our situation by assessing the needs of our students. We quickly discovered that test scores indicated approximately 60 percent of our student population was below grade level in mathematics and reading. After much discussion about how to address this problem, we decided that an after-school tutorial program would help these students, so we set about designing it, with the full support of our district leadership.

One of our concerns was how to acquire funding for the program. The budget planning cycle for the district had passed and no funds were available, so external funding from a grant was necessary. We conducted a funding search, identified a potential funder, and contacted that organization. The grant proposal was developed and submitted, and we received the grant.

Getting that grant made such a difference in our school! We were able to set up a one-year program that included additional reading and math instruction on alternating afternoons. The grant gave us the funds to pay for an extra school-bus run to take the tutorial students home, stipends for our teachers, and money for high-interest reading and math materials.

Did I mention that this was a volunteer situation for teachers? And that every teacher in the school volunteered? We celebrated our achievements throughout the year, and wonderful things began to happen. Non-readers became readers, grades started to rise, there were fewer discipline problems and less absenteeism. Parents supported the program and appreciated our efforts. In addition, our year-end testing results were excellent.

Some people made a big deal about that, but what really mattered to us was the change in our students. This wasn't the first grant proposal I had written, but it is one of the grants I remember most fondly. The grant-writing process of identifying the need, gaining support from the district, acquiring funding, developing the proposal, and implementing the program felt like a minor effort compared to what we accomplished.

As a teacher, principal, or district-level supervisor, you are committed to providing your students with the best possible education, but often you do not have the funding necessary to do so. As education budgets become tighter and tighter, the way to obtain money for many worthwhile projects is often through developing grant proposals that can be submitted to federal, state, or private funding sources.

Over the past twenty-five years, I have taught grant writing to thousands of teachers, counselors, and school administrators. This book is written specifically for teachers and school administrators who want to understand this process. We begin with some of the questions that educators ask about grant writing. Following these basic questions, the eight steps of the process are outlined and discussed.

By reviewing the entire process at the beginning of your journey, you will be able to see how later information fits into each of the eight steps. Sometimes a large grant isn't necessary — perhaps a teacher or administrator requires only a few hundred dollars for a small class or school project. We'll discuss how to ask for these smaller grants as well as how to apply for the larger, more formal grants. The appendix contains a number of helpful resources, such as a glossary of grant-writing terms, an extensive grant-writing resource section that includes many online and hard-copy resources, a sample federal grant proposal, a sample local government application, a sample foundation grant, and a grant-writing rubric to help you develop and evaluate your own grant proposals.

Educators, as a group, do not compete for available funds as effectively as do other organizations and nonprofits. Perhaps a significant reason teachers and administrators don't write more grant proposals is that we are extremely busy with the day-to-day duties of schooling students. Another reason is that many educators have not been exposed to the act of grant writing and may be intimidated by the process or not understand it. Grant writing is a process too seldom taught in many pre-service or graduate education courses.

It has been my experience that teachers and school administrators can become excellent grant writers. With basic knowledge and a little practice, educators can and do develop grant proposals to fund projects that address the unmet needs of their students. It is professionally and personally rewarding when your funded project/program has a positive impact on the lives of your students. The time spent on a grant proposal is well worth it when compared to the benefits received from a well-designed and well-implemented project/program. To those of you who have never written a grant, be encouraged. Your skills as a grant writer will grow with practice. To those of you who have written a grant and received funding, you know the satisfaction of which I speak. I encourage each of you to use the information in this book to address the needs of your students through grant writing. When you receive a grant, please take a moment and send me an email. It makes my day. Good luck, and best wishes with your grant-writing efforts.

B. SLIGER
www.grantwriting.com

## Chapter 1

Questions about Grant Writing

I HAVE worked with thousands of educators over the past twenty-five years and have been asked countless questions regarding grant writing. Because many of these same questions pop up time and time again, I have listed several of the most common ones below to serve as an introduction to the grant-writing process.

What can grants be used for?

Grants can be used to support/supplement education by:

- Enhancing or sustaining existing educational programs/ projects
- Developing new programs
- Purchasing equipment/technology
- Funding construction projects
- Hiring personnel
- Developing curriculum
- Promoting professional development
- Most educational grants are written for a project that reflects any one of the above areas.

How much money is available?

There are more than 70,000 foundations (the number increases each year) in the United States, and they provided more than $40 billion in grants in 2007. (The amount has increased each year for the past several years.) Wealthy individuals also give away billions of dollars each year. Nearly one-fourth of all foundation money is given under the category of Education; in total, twenty-six federal agencies gave away more than $400 billion in 2007. The U.S. Department of Education provided more than $36 billion to states and school districts to improve K–12 schools and meet the needs of students.

Each federal agency has dozens of grant opportunities available at different times during the fiscal year. The amounts of individual grants vary, but billions of dollars are provided annually by the federal government in the form of grants. As of this writing, the Department of Education has more than one hundred grant opportunities. Be sure to check out their Web site: www.ed.gov/funding.

Will my school or district qualify for a grant?

Yes, school districts qualify for grants like nonprofit organizations with 501(c)(3) status. This is good news since this tax status is a requirement of most funding sources.

Why do some school districts receive more grants than others?

Some school districts do a better job of seeking and obtaining grants than others. Some districts have a grants office with a full-time grant writer. I have found that districts that hire a full-time grant writer bring in anywhere from one million to several million dollars in grant funds each year. The grant writer works with teachers and administrators who are developing educational projects to meet the needs of their students and district and thus becomes familiar with their district's requirements and priorities. Then the grant writer helps to locate appropriate funding sources for grants developed by teachers and other school or district personnel. These grant writers usually oversee the various grant programs throughout the district and make sure that grant funds are expended according to the terms of each grant proposal. Managing grant funds is an important task in itself.

In other school districts, grant writing is another "hat" that someone at the district office wears. This person is usually so involved with other duties that grant writing takes a backseat. In fact, some districts seldom seek grant funds at all.

Most school districts fall between the two extremes. A few years ago, a superintendent attending one of my workshops said with a grin, "So many teachers and administrators are writing and receiving grants that I had to hire another bookkeeper to keep it all straight." Not a bad situation to be in.

Can teachers and other school/district leaders write grants?

Yes! This book is dedicated to helping you do just that. Teachers and other school leaders can be very effective grant writers. You have the necessary knowledge and skills, as well as a firsthand understanding of student needs. You have been trained to work with students in a PK–12 educational setting and can quickly identify the areas in which your students require help. Identifying the need is an important first step for grant writers.

This book will help you understand the grant-writing process by going through it one step at a time. Once you understand the process, you will be well on your way to being a successful grant writer. That means you will be able to use your newfound knowledge to acquire funding for worthwhile programs and projects to address the needs of your students.

I began writing grants more than twenty-five years ago, and I still get excited about the process. When you see firsthand the results that a well-thought-out program or project has on the lives and educational achievement of students it is personally and professionally rewarding. You know that without the grant none of it would have been possible, which keeps you motivated to write grant after grant. That is not to say that all of your projects will be funded—some will, some won't. However, the more you learn about the process, the better at it you will become. As we tell our students, "Practice makes perfect."

What are my chances?

Good! Money is available; the challenge is knowing where it is and how to go about getting it. When I was a first-year elementary school principal, the faculty decided that integrating technology into our curriculum was an important priority that was not being addressed. We decided to seek funding for this project by developing a grant proposal and contacting possible funding sources to help make our dream a reality. Our dream did become a reality. We received a grant that allowed us to purchase hardware and several thousand dollars' worth of educational software. Our students benefited greatly from our efforts, which made us grateful and proud.

However, grant writing is not without its disappointments. There are no guarantees. Fortunately, the more you learn about the process, the more likely you are to receive a call or letter telling you that your proposal has been funded. Persistence is a necessary trait for a successful grant writer.

What exactly is a grant, and could you explain other grant-writing jargon?

Here are some grant-related terms you need to know:

- **Grant**: An award of funds, services, or materials to be used for the specific activities described in the grant proposal.

- **Applicant**: The person submitting a grant proposal to a funding source. Most people think of a grant as an award of funds. However, a grant can also consist of services or equipment donated to your organization. When I was an elementary principal, we had an active volunteer program in our school—parents and community leaders worked in various capacities. In one program, thirty trained and screened volunteers tutored students in reading. If we had had to pay for these services, the program would have been quite costly. Thankfully, a service grant helped many of our kids.

- **Funding Source (Funder)**: Can be a corporation; a foundation; a business; a federal, state, or local agency; or an

4

individual. Chapter Three of this book will discuss in detail each type of funding source. Keep in mind that any time you see "funder" or "funding source" in this book it refers to federal agencies, state and local governments, foundations, corporations, businesses, and/or wealthy individuals.

- **Project Director**: The individual responsible for the funded project, who makes sure the project is implemented as stated in the grant proposal. The project director is the contact person for the funding source but does not have to be the same person who wrote the grant. Your school might want to establish a grant-writing team that develops various grant proposals to meet school needs. The project director could easily be someone who is not on the team but who will oversee a project if it is funded.

- **Grantee**: The individual or organization receiving a grant, who is responsible or accountable for it. If the grantee receives the grant, then the "grantor" (funding source) is the federal or state agency, foundation, corporation, other nonprofit organization, or individual awarding a grant to the recipient.

These basic terms are enough to get us started. Appendix A (page 71) includes a full glossary of grant terms that will be very helpful to you.

How do you develop fundable ideas?

There are two basic approaches:

- Find a fashionable funding area. With this approach, you determine what types of programs/projects funding agencies have funded in the past and what they are currently funding. Use that information to guide the development of your grant proposal.

- Brainstorm about the needs of your school district, school, and/or students. Consider what program or project could be developed to address those needs, and discuss your idea with people who can provide you with good feedback, such as colleagues, community leaders, parents, and even students. Then search out potential funders.

Keep in mind that a need exists whenever there is a difference between what is and what could be. Identifying the need is a critical first step in the grant-writing process. Personally, I favor the second approach in developing a fundable idea. Sometimes both approaches are addressed by a grant idea.

How long do grants last?

It depends on your program/project and the funding agency's guidelines. Foundations and corporations tend to fund programs/projects for one fiscal year. A teacher might develop a summer camp for science students that lasts three weeks, or a group of teachers may develop a literacy program that lasts the entire school year. In both cases, the program or project would be completed within a one-year period of time.

Are there multi-year grants?

Yes, most of which are state- or federal-agency grants. The application materials for a state or federal grant will let you know if the grant is for a one-, two-, or even three-year period of time. Some foundations and corporations also provide multi-year funding.

Are grant projects/programs ever funded more than once by the same source?

They can be. Most grants are funded for up to one fiscal year. However, if the funder sees results and is supportive of the program/project, they may continue to fund it year after year. This is the exception, not the rule.

What is a funding search?

Determining a funding source for a project or program is a critical component of the grant-writing process. There are several possible sources of grant funds: federal agencies, state and local agencies, foundations, corporations, local businesses, and wealthy in-dividuals. The purpose of a funding search is to locate a funder who will provide financial support for your project or program. By researching individual funders, you will determine which ones are most likely to fund a project or program like yours. In Chapter Three we will discuss some of the resources available in conducting a funding search.

What is a grant proposal?

The grant proposal is a formal written document that provides detailed information to a funding source or funder about the proposed implementation and cost of a specific program or project.

What are the components of a grant proposal?

The main components of a grant proposal are:

- Cover Letter
- Title Page
- Table of Contents
- Abstract (Executive Summary)
- Classroom/School/District Background
- Needs Statement
- Program/Project Description
  - Goal(s)
  - Objectives
  - Project Activities
  - Project Timeline
  - Evaluation
- Budget
- Appendix

Think of a grant proposal as a puzzle or story. Each piece of the puzzle or story has a job to do, and when they are put to-gether effectively the puzzle or story is complete. Funders will have different grant-component requirements. Some funders will ask for only a few of the above components in a grant proposal; others will require all of them. Chapter Four will discuss in detail the components of an effective grant proposal.

How much money can you receive from a grant?

Individual grants range in size from a few hundred to several million dollars. Some teachers just want a small grant for a classroom program. Others may require hundreds of thousands of dollars for an extensive district project. Chapters Two through Five discuss the process of large-grant acquisition. Chapter Six explains the process for acquiring a small grant (a few hundred to a few thousand dollars).

Is the process different for large grants and small grants?

Yes. Large grants can range from a few thousand to several million dollars. Small grants can range from a few hundred to one or two thousand dollars. Proposals for large grants are usually more involved and require more time to prepare. Small grants are often, but not always, obtained from local sources such as businesses or individuals in a community. Chapters Two through Five focus on large grants; Chapter Six deals with the process of small-grant attainment.

What is a 501(c)(3)?

This is a designation provided to tax-exempt organizations by the Internal Revenue Service. Organizations that are eligible for tax-exempt status are nonprofit in nature (religious organizations, schools, libraries, service organizations, hospitals, public charities, etc.). The vast majority of funding sources require that the recipient have nonprofit status in order to receive grant funds.

What is the difference between a letter of intent and a letter of inquiry?

A letter of intent is a letter sent by a grantee (you) to a funding source (usually a federal agency or a foundation) stating your intention to submit a grant proposal. Some federal agencies and foundations require a letter of intent. A letter of inquiry, which is also sent by a grantee to a funding source, contains a brief description or overview of a proposed project or program to see if the funding source is interested in funding the project.

What is a letter of support?

Letters of endorsement and support should be written by significant individuals in your school, school district, and community who have had an opportunity to review your grant proposal. They are writing a letter in support of your grant program, indicating that you have identified a true need and that they believe your proposal will address that need. A generic letter of support is not as effective as a specific letter tailored to the funding source. This is a very important part of your grant proposal. Depending on the focus of your grant, you might obtain letters of support from your school administration, other teachers, associate superintendent, superintendent, board members, PTA/PTO president, or appropriate community leaders.

How important is the budget?

Your project/program budget is a critical component of your grant proposal. The budget will explain to the funding source how monies will be spent to accomplish the goal(s), objectives, and activities of your program/project. Chapter Four will provide an in-depth look at budget development.

After I submit a grant proposal, how soon will I hear something?

This varies. Each funding source has its own timeframe for reviewing grant proposals and notifying the grantee. Notification guidelines are usually learned during the funding search. This is explained in more detail in Chapter Three.

Can I resubmit a grant proposal to another funder if it has been turned down?

Yes; a subsequent funder may think your grant proposal is a great idea. There are many funding sources, and they have different areas of focus. This is one of the exciting aspects of grant writing.

Should I provide some type of recognition for the funder if I receive the grant?

Yes, unless the funder requests otherwise. Most funders will appreciate your efforts to provide appropriate recognition for their organization. This can be done in many ways, such as a newspaper article written by the grantee or a newspaper reporter, thank-you notes written by your students, a special lunch honoring the funder, an award ceremony, etc. If your efforts involve public recognition, let the funder know what you are planning to make sure they approve.

Is there a lot of information on the Internet about grants?

The Internet has a wealth of resources and will be a tremendous asset to your grant-writing efforts. The Internet can assist you in conducting research for your proposed project or program, from need identification and documentation to locating sources of funding. Make sure you review Appendix B for a list of many outstanding Web sites.

What are matching funds? How do they work?

Some funders require that the grantee contribute to the project/program by matching all or some portion of the funds provided by the funding source. The match can either be "soft" (in-kind) money or "hard" (actual dollars) money. See Chapter Four for more information concerning the budget.

I've heard that I have to use "buzz" words to obtain grants—is that true?

Contrary to what you may have heard, do not use "buzz" words in your grant proposal. It is more important that you clearly convey to the funding source that you have identified a true need and have a plan for addressing that need in your proposal.

If my grant is turned down, should I ask the funder why?

Yes. Some funders will provide you with valuable feedback on your proposal, and you might gain insight into how they review proposals. Other funders will not provide feedback. It does not hurt to ask, but make sure you do so in a non-defensive way. The next time you submit a proposal to this same funder, keep in mind what was shared with you. If you believe their suggestions were helpful, retool your proposal and send it to another funding source. However, do not resubmit the same proposal to the same funder unless you are told to do so.

Is it true that some foundations, corporations, and government agencies have a grant application for grantees to fill out?

Yes. Some funding sources require that grantees fill out an application rather than provide an original grant proposal. Many applications are available online at the Web sites for foundations, corporations, and government agencies. The grant components of an online or paper application will be the same or very similar to the components of a grant proposal. Some applications will limit the length of your response in each section, so your answers must be clear and concise. See Appendix D for a sample local government grant application.

What is an RFP?

An RFP (request for proposal) is an invitation from a funding source, usually a federal agency or a foundation, detailing what the source will fund, who can apply, and their application procedures and deadlines. The grantee reviews the RFP and determines whether or not to submit a grant proposal. Federal agencies issue RFPs all the time. Check out www.grant.gov to view hundreds of grant opportunities.

11

How important is the sustainability of a program/project?

The capability to continue a project/program when the funding runs out is important to some funders. You might need to address sustainability in your grant proposal if this is a criterion of the funding source. Some level of project/program continuation after the funding ends might be enough to satisfy the funding source. For example, if a grant is funded to help elementary students improve their reading, and part of the grant's budget is spent on high-interest reading materials, a case can be made that after the program ends the reading materials will continue to be used to help other students. Make sure you explain how those materials will continue to be used.

What is a 990-PF?

Foundations must file a 990-PF (private foundation) form with the Internal Revenue Service. This form provides a great deal of information to the grant seeker about the foundation, such as recipients of the foundation's grants and how much was provided. You can access foundation 990s through GuideStar (www.guidestar.org) and the Foundation Center (www.foundationcenter.org).

What about the use of educational jargon?

Be very careful when using educational terminology. Whenever you use a word or phrase in your proposal that a reader may not understand, define it immediately. Grant reviewers tend to have a business background and are not always familiar with educational jargon. For the sake of clarity, define or explain educational terms and ideas.

What is a grant-writing team?

A grant-writing team is a group of educators working together on a grant proposal to capitalize on the knowledge and experience of each group member. A team can consist of teachers and/or administrators from the same school. A district-level team works together on district-level projects. Research on group dynamics indicates that an effective team of individuals working on a common task is almost always more productive and produces a better product than one person working alone.

If you have the opportunity to work with other colleagues on a proposal, it can be professionally and personally rewarding. However, one person on the team needs to lead the process and edit the proposal to make sure it flows. If people are working on different parts of the proposal and the pieces are put together without careful editing, the proposal will have serious problems. It's not necessary that a proposal be done by a group; most proposals are written by only one person. Depending on your situation, you may or may not want or need to work as a group.

Chapter 2

The Grant-Writing Process

LET'S BEGIN by thinking of grant writing as a process with generally accepted steps or procedures. I say "generally accepted" because there is no single way of obtaining grants, yet there are common practices or approaches utilized by most grant writers. Knowing these steps or procedures will greatly increase the probability that your grant will be funded. This chapter will help you understand the basic process of grant writing that has been used successfully by me and thousands of other educators to obtain grants for worthwhile educational projects and programs. Figure 1 (page 17) provides a visual overview of the entire grant-writing process. Take a moment to review each step in Figure 1 to give you a feel for the process. Briefly, the eight steps are as follows:

1. Identify a need that is not currently being met or not being met well. Determine if you or your team can develop a plan to address the need.

2. Obtain documentation from as many sources as possible indicating that the need exists.

3. Discuss this need and your ideas about how to address it with the appropriate school and district leaders. Acquire support to continue with the grant-writing process.

4. Begin your search for a potential funding source to whom you will send your proposal.

5. Contact the funding source.

6. Develop your proposal based on the funding source's criteria.

7. Submit your grant proposal by the deadline, if there is one.

8. Follow up with the funding source.

Sometimes there are variations in the process. However, knowing these basic steps will serve you well. Each step is summarized below, and some of the steps are discussed in greater detail in Chapters Three, Four, and Five.

Identify the Need

I cannot overemphasize the importance of this first step in the grant-writing process. As a teacher or school leader, you are in a position to identify the needs of your students and to know whether or not there are enough funds available from your system to address those needs.

This first step in the process can be both challenging and exciting for a grant writer. It's an opportunity to brainstorm ideas for addressing your students' specific needs. I have found that working with other teachers can increase the impact and effectiveness of the brainstorming process. A group of individuals working together on a common focus usually results in a better solution than one person working alone. When I work with schools and districts, I suggest that a grant-writing team be established whenever possible. It is personally and professionally rewarding to work with colleagues on a grant proposal; you gain the benefit of varied ideas and experiences, and you can delegate work rather than doing it all yourself. If you have the opportunity to form a grant-writing team in your school or district, please consider the rewards of doing so.

Once you have identified an unmet need, you must formulate a plan to address it. Think of a need as the difference between what is and what could be. Your project or program will focus

16

Figure 1

The Grant-Writing Process

on reducing the gap between what currently is and where you would like your students to be after the program or project has ended. You must explain to the funding source why your project or program is needed and provide any and all pertinent documentation. In Chapter Four, we will look more closely at documenting an identified need.

Make sure you spend an adequate amount of time thinking about the need you want to address with your grant proposal. Funding sources look carefully at your identified need, and you must ensure that your need matches the funding agency's criteria. This is a critical part of your grant proposal and a crucial first step in the grant-writing process.

Document the Need

There are several ways to document an identified need. One is to conduct a needs assessment, which can be administered to students, parents, teachers, and other people in the community. The information gathered from the needs assessment can be used to support the need that you have identified.

Another way to document a need is to use statistical data. For example, you might refer to students' test scores or demographic data from your school or community. A third option is to conduct a brief literature review. Finally, surveys can be administered to students, teachers, parents, and members of the community to gather data that supports your identified need. Each of these techniques will be discussed in more detail in Chapter Four. Just keep in mind that it is not enough to say you have a need. You must provide supporting documentation to the funding source to show that a true need exists.

Discuss the Need with Colleagues, and Obtain Approval

The third step in the grant-writing process is to discuss your identified need and your idea for addressing that need with appropriate school personnel. If you are a teacher, you will want to discuss the idea with your school principal and obtain approval to continue with the grant-writing process. The principal might need to submit the grant idea to the appropriate office at the county or district level for approval. This process of approval is different for each school district. You must find out what the process is in your district.

One school I worked with had a process that was quite involved. The teacher had to acquire permission to work on the grant from the principal, the principal had to obtain approval from the district's grant office, the grant office required approval from the associate superintendent, and the associate superintendent had to get approval from the superintendent. Finally, the superintendent had to gain permission from the local board of education before the grant could be submitted to the funding source. This process took anywhere from two to three months to complete. If you are in a school or district that does not require this many levels of approval, count yourself lucky. In some school districts the teacher simply discusses the proposed project with the school principal, and once the principal has given the go-ahead the teacher is free to work through the rest of the grant-writing process. Be sure you follow your county or district's procedure for submitting grant proposals to outside funding agencies. In many cases, school administrators and district-level leaders can provide resources and suggestions about how to improve and develop a program or project to meet the identified need.

Teachers are looked upon favorably by their school leaders for writing grants to address the needs of their students. However, skipping Step Three in the grant-writing process can turn a good plan into an undesirable situation for a well-intentioned teacher. I remember an instance in which a teacher was so excited about writing a grant proposal for her class that she skipped this step and submitted her proposal to the funding source without first seeking approval. A few weeks later, the funding officer from the foundation contacted the school principal with questions regarding the budget for the grant proposal. Needless to say, the principal was unaware of the proposal and was not pleased with the teacher. The funding source did not fund the grant, and the students did not benefit from a worthwhile project. All of this could have been avoided if the teacher had simply followed the grant-writing process and gotten the proper approval.

Conduct the Funding Search

Who are the potential funding sources for your projects/programs? In no particular order, possible funders include:

- Foundations
- Corporations
- Federal agencies
- State and local agencies
- Local businesses
- Wealthy individuals

In Chapter Three I will go into detail about each of these sources. In most cases you will identify so many places to send your grant proposal that you will simply not have time to apply to all of them. *It is critical that you conduct a very careful search of po-*

tential funding sources. You must identify (through your research) those funders that might actually fund your project/program. You are wasting your time—and the funder's—by sending a proposal that does not meet their criteria. For example, if a source funds only medical research and your grant is for an after-school literacy program, it will not have a chance of being funded. Do your homework!

Contact the Potential Funder

If, based on your research, your project meets the funding source's criteria, you are ready for the next step. Contact the funding agency by making a phone call or writing a letter of inquiry. A letter of inquiry is very important when contacting foundations and corporations. However, if you call the funding source, you can often find out whom to send your proposal to, any specific guidelines that are required in the proposal, and the proposal review cycle (the dates when the funding source will review proposals). Also, verify the mailing address and find out the name of the current funding officer. Do not rely on Web sites and print resources—they can be outdated. You do not want to send your proposal to a funding officer who left the position three weeks ago.

Develop the Proposal

Next, you'll need to develop your proposal and tailor it to the criteria of the funding agency. Chapter Four will detail the components of an effective grant proposal.

Submit Your Grant Proposal to the Funding Source

Some foundations review proposals each month, others every three months, some twice a year, and a few only once a year. Use your knowledge of review-cycle dates to help you determine which funding source to send your proposal to first. If your grant will sit on a reviewer's desk for the next few months, you might want to send it to another source with a closer review date first. If that source doesn't fund it, you can send your proposal to a funder with a later review date. In all cases, submit your proposal to the funding agency before their review deadline. Keep a log or record of potential funders, the dates you contacted them, the name of the person you talked to, any information they shared with you, their review-cycle dates, when you submitted your proposal, and how and when you followed up.

Follow Up

After the funding agency reviews your proposal, they will almost certainly have questions for you. Be prepared to follow up and clarify as needed.

If your grant is approved, send a letter of appreciation to the funder. Even if you are not approved, send that letter. It is a courteous thing to do, it reflects well on you professionally, and it might even get a source to reconsider. One teacher I know was not approved for a grant that she applied for. She wrote such a nice letter of appreciation to the funding officer thanking him for considering her project that he went back, pulled out her proposal, reread it, and decided to fund that project after all. It doesn't happen often…but you never know.

Many times your proposal will not be funded on the first go-round. You might need to submit two or three different proposals to the same funding source before your project or program is approved. Each time, write a letter of appreciation thanking the funder for their time and consideration. Most funding agencies keep a record of all grant submissions. When funders check your file and see that follow-up letter, it reflects well on you and your professionalism.

Another vital aspect of the follow-up step is managing an awarded grant. Received funds must be spent according to the specifications in the grant proposal. Significant changes in the program/project design and/or the budget must be approved by the funding source. Requested changes should be done in writing; if you call to request a change, you must follow up with a written request. A reasonable request is usually approved by the funder. For example, at the end of the grant program/project you might have a few hundred dollars left over because you did such a good job managing the project funds. You could make a request to the funder, asking to spend that money to support your project in a legitimate way that was not included on the original proposal.

Maintain all grant funds in a separate account, and keep receipts of all expenditures. The good news is that when you are awarded a grant, the funds will not be sent directly to you—they will go to your district's accounting office. You will make requests of that office whenever you need to expend grant funds for your project. Records of expenditures will be kept for you. Of course you will want to monitor your expenditures and account balance throughout the grant project. Remember, you must spend your grant dollars according to the specifications laid out in your grant proposal.

Chapter 3

Conducting a Funding Search

EVERYBODY WANTS them, but where do you find grants?

In this chapter, we will discuss some of the excellent resources available to you in your funding search. Knowing that these resources exist—and how to utilize them—can greatly increase your chances of receiving funding for your educational project or program. I have included a complete bibliography of these and other resources in Appendix B. Remember: the purpose of these resources is to help you match your program/project with a potential funding source. This can take time, but it is necessary in order to increase your chances of being funded.

This chapter is an in-depth look at Step Four in the grant-writing process. Grants can be obtained from the federal government, state and local governments, foundations and corporations, local businesses, and even wealthy individuals. As an educator, you must be familiar with each of these possible funding sources.

Federal Grants

The federal government provides billions of dollars each year in the form of grants. Federal grants can be classified in two ways: direct grants or pass-through grants. Direct grants are monies received directly from the federal agency (no middleman). Pass-through grants are federal monies given to states for distribution.

The state agency then decides who will receive the federal money. Grantees (you) apply directly to the federal agency for a direct grant. For pass-through grants, you apply to the appropriate state agency for the federal funds.

Every federal agency has its own budget as appropriated and approved by Congress, and each agency has many grant programs. For example, as of this writing, the Department of Education has more than a hundred grant programs. There are several ways to find out about federal grant programs. Each federal agency provides an RFP (Request for Proposal) whenever grant funds are available.

Let's take a look at how this process works. Each federal agency requests funds from Congress. Congress approves an agency's budget. Let's suppose that the Department of Education has determined that an alternative education program for high school students might significantly reduce the dropout rate. The agency issues an RFP providing information about the new program, including who is eligible to apply for the grant, the deadline for the grant submission, how much money will be awarded, criteria for submissions, agency contact information, and other information. After reviewing the RFP, school districts determine whether or not they are going to develop a grant proposal for submission.

There are several ways to find out about RFPs for government grants. One of the best ways is to visit the Web site www.grants.gov, which provides access to all the grant opportunities from twenty-six federal agencies, including the Department of Education. More than 1,000 RFPs are available on this site. Please take some time to visit and explore the site. With a little practice, you will be able to search several agencies to determine if federal grant monies are available for your project. You can even register on the Web site to receive notification of grant opportunities.

The Department of Education will be the most obvious place to search for federal education monies. However, several other agencies also provide grant funds for educational projects and programs. Also, some federal agencies have initiatives that are funded year after year. With new initiatives (grant programs) made available each year, it behooves grant writers seeking federal funds to constantly monitor funding opportunities from several federal agencies.

Another resource for finding federal grant opportunities is the Federal Register, which is published by the United States Government Printing Office. It's the federal government's way of keeping citizens informed about what is going on in each of the federal programs. All grant opportunities must be listed in the Federal Register before being announced in any other place. The Federal Register can be searched online at www.ed.gov/legislation/FedRegister/announcements/index.html. Most large libraries maintain a section of government documents that includes electronic access to the Federal Register. Keep in mind that by the time a local library receives the Register, some of the grant opportunities may have expired or enough time may have passed that it is impossible to prepare a grant proposal in time to meet the deadline.

Another excellent resource for finding federal money is the Catalog of Federal Domestic Assistance (CFDA). I have conducted grant-writing workshops for many years throughout the United States, and I always ask participants if they have heard about this publication. In a large room, maybe one or two hands go up, but often there are none. The CFDA is published by the U.S. Government Printing Office each year. It contains all the grant opportunities for each federal agency. This is a great place to search for federal grant monies. You can locate federal programs that offer grant funds for projects like yours. Keep in mind that the information in the CFDA is dated, so you will need to go online to www.grants.gov or check the specific agency's Web site for current information. When looking for federal funds, I review the CFDA to see if I can find a federal program similar to my project. Then I go to www.grants.gov for current info on that program or check the agency's Web site and review the RFP for that particular program. After reviewing the RFP, you must decide whether or not to apply for the funds. (See Appendix C for a sample federal grant proposal.) Keep in mind that different federal agencies have their own application packages or guidelines that need to be followed to the letter.

Even though federal grants require more effort than other sources of grant funding, the benefits of receiving a federal grant can make all the work worthwhile. It is crucial to review an RFP very carefully before beginning a federal grant proposal. Review the RFP two or three times and take notes about important points. Make sure to follow the guidelines exactly. Points will be deducted, or your proposal may be rejected, if you do not follow the guidelines precisely. For many grant programs, you can complete your application package online. This saves paper and ensures that your application is received before the required deadline; mail can occasionally be delayed or lost.

Federal grant proposals are usually the most challenging to write. They range in length from a few pages to more than a hundred pages, depending on the program. It can take a great deal of time to put together a federal grant proposal, but the effort can be well worth it since federal grants tend to be large, ranging from several thousand to even millions of dollars.

State and Local Grants

State and local governments occasionally provide grant monies to schools and school districts. The types of grants available for educational projects vary from state to state. You can locate possible funding opportunities by searching the Web or making a few phone calls. Your first stop for education grants should be your state's Department of Education.

State and local agencies have their own application packages. As always, review an application very carefully before you start working on the proposal. Make sure to follow all instructions and guidelines exactly. If you have any questions, contact the office that is overseeing the grant opportunity.

Usually, state and local grants are easier to obtain than federal grants. Remember that state agencies sometimes handle pass-through grants from the federal government. These pass-through grants can be medium to large grants.

State grants are almost always larger than local grants, but local grants are easier to obtain. Local grants are made available through local government agencies. Local officials are usually aware of the needs in their community, so a well-designed grant proposal addressing a need of children in a local school has a good chance of being funded. (Appendix D includes a copy of a sample local grant application. Take a moment to review it; the application will give you an idea of what may be required for a local grant.) Sometimes applications or notifications of small grant opportunities are placed in teachers' mailboxes. The agencies supporting these small grants usually fund several of them. They range anywhere from a few hundred dollars to one to two thousand dollars each. Chapter Six includes more information about finding small grants.

Grants from Foundations and Corporations

Foundations and corporations give away billions of dollars every year. There are more than 70,000 foundations in the United States, with new ones forming each year. Some foundations have been around for several decades. A foundation can be defined as a non-profit, non-governmental organization that provides other organizations with grants. The first foundations came into existence more than two hundred years ago. Some are set up by wealthy individuals, families, or corporations. There are small foundations, which give away only a few hundred to a few thousand dollars per applicant, midsize foundations, and large foundations that provide more sizable grants.

Foundations are required by law to give away at least five percent of their earnings each year in the form of grants. Foundations invest their funds in stocks, bonds, and other investments in order to earn interest. If the economy is doing well, the amount of funds given away is greater that year. Every foundation has its own area of interest. Some focus on educational programs and projects, while others focus on health, medical research, or other areas. When foundations are part of your funding search, be sure that education (K–12) is one of their areas of interest before you apply.

Some foundations are known as family foundations; the funds to start the foundation were provided by a wealthy family. Sometimes members of the family oversee the funding of grants. There are also community foundations, which focus their giving in a certain geographic area. Most foundations are private. Controlled by a board of directors, these foundations give away the most grant money, so the majority of your efforts will focus on private foundations.

Do your homework before sending your proposal to a foundation. During your funding search, focus only on foundations whose area of interest matches your project or program, and make sure that your proposal meets the funding agency's criteria. Review the agency's grant application guidelines, and narrow your list to those foundations that fit all your requirements. If your project requires a $50,000 grant and the average-size grant the foundation provides is $10,000, you are probably wasting your time. Also, corporate foundations typically provide grants only to organizations within the geographic area of the corporation—something else to keep in mind.

Once you have narrowed your list, contact the foundation. A phone call is a good way to start. Begin by introducing yourself and asking a few basic questions, such as the name of the current funding officer and their mailing address. Request any materials that might help you prepare your proposal, and ask for suggestions or information that might be pertinent.

When you call, you might speak with the foundation secretary or even the funding officer. The funding officer is hired by the board of directors; his or her job is to help coordinate the foundation's financial gifts. The funding officer reads grant proposals and often makes recommendations to the board of directors. If you are asked about your project, briefly explain the main purpose of your grant. If the foundation is local, ask if you can make an appointment to discuss your project with the funding officer. Sometimes funding officers will meet with potential grantees, but not always. If you are submitting your grant to a foundation that is not local, a face-to-face meeting will not be expected. Your sole contact with the funding officer will be by mail, e-mail, or phone. In some cases, you will simply submit your proposal to the foundation and wait to hear from them.

During your funding search of foundations, note when the board of directors meets to vote on grant proposals. You won't know if your proposal has been funded until after the board meets. Some boards meet monthly, some quarterly, and others only once or twice a year. I suggest you develop a schedule for the submission of your grant proposals to remind yourself about board of directors meeting dates, when and whom you have submitted proposals to, and any feedback you received from the funding source, as well as whom you talked with at the foundation and the date of contact.

How do you find foundations? How do you find out their areas of interest? When do the board of directors meets? How much money do they give away? Their average-size grant? Where they are located? Their contact information? What kind of support they provide? Any limitations to their giving? Let's take a look at some of the excellent resources professional grant writers use to find answers to all of these questions and more.

The Internet provides access to many grant-writing resources, including foundations. I have included an extensive list of grant-writing resources, both online and print, in Appendix B. Some especially helpful resources are listed here:

The Foundation Center: The Foundation Center's Web site (www.fdcenter.org) is an excellent place to start your funding search. The Foundation Center is recognized as a leader in resources for grant writers. It provides grantees access to foundations, charities, and corporations that provide grants, and it maintains large searchable databases on each potential funder. A great deal of information, much of it free, regarding the many aspects of grant writing is available at this site. You can sign up for a free newsletter that will help keep you informed of possible funding opportunities. The newsletter is particularly helpful to educators. In addition to their online resources, the Foundation Center also publishes a great deal of printed material and provides it to libraries across the United States. You can find those libraries on their Web site; visit a library to review more materials to assist you in your funding efforts.

Note: Foundations must submit a 990-PF form to the IRS each year. This form contains valuable information about grants funded by the foundation, detailing who received a grant from the foundation and for how much. Make sure to review these forms during your funding search. GuideStar (www.GuideStar.org) and The Foundation Center (www.fdcenter.org) will allow you to review 990-PF forms (see Appendix B).

WestED: A nonprofit research, development, and service agency, WestEd (www.wested.org) enhances and increases education and human development within schools, families, and communities. It offers a listing of corporate and foundation grant sources. Make sure you check out their Guide to Grants section.

Thompson Publishing Group: This Web site (www.thompson.com) provides information on foundation and federal grant opportunities and has several worthwhile listings for those seeking funding for educational programs.

Many more sites are listed in Appendix B. When you begin to explore these resources (online and print) they will provide you with information such as:

- The name of the foundation/corporation
- Its address and phone number
- Size of grants given
- The purpose and activities of the foundation/corporation
- Fields of interest, such as education, hospitals, cultural programs, etc.
- Types of support given, such as seed money, capital campaigns, building funds, etc.
- Limitations; for example, no grants to individuals, no scholarships, applications not accepted, only give to pre-selected organizations, etc.
- Application information, such as how many copies of your proposal to submit, their notification date, board meeting dates, if an application form is not required, etc.
- Deadlines for submission
- Sample grants, or a brief description of previously funded grants

Review each foundation or corporation entry and decide if there is a match between your needs and the funder's interests. *This is a critical step.* The better the match, the more likely it is that you will receive a grant. Do not try to force a fit; instead, go on to the next entry, and the next, until one jumps out at you. Make a list of organizations to contact.

Grants from Local Businesses

Local businesses can be an excellent source of funds for many grant projects/programs. Local banks, factories/plants, and large retail stores underwrite community affairs, so they are often willing to support worthwhile educational projects/programs. Personal contact with a local businessperson is critical to your success.

Many medium to large local factories or businesses have a budget for community support. A plant manager may have the discretion to donate up to $10,000 for a project without approval from the home office. The amount varies from company to company.

If you receive a grant from a local business, it is very important to provide appropriate recognition for their contributions. Possible ways to recognize the funder are through a newspaper article explaining the project and who made it possible, having your students write thank-you cards, or hosting a special lunch ceremony.

Grants from Wealthy Individuals

Wealthy individuals give away billions of dollars each year to charities. Some of these individuals are interested in assisting educators by funding projects/programs to help kids. As a school principal, I approached a local wealthy individual about a school project. He said that he had lived in the community for twenty-five years, and I was the first educator to come to him with a request. He facetiously asked if we (the educators) had all the money we needed, since no one had asked for his help before.

It is true that most educators don't think about asking wealthy individuals to help out with worthwhile projects, yet many other organizations both in and out of a community do not hesitate to make requests. Consider exploring this avenue. Of course, as with all requests, get approval from your school district first, then conduct a search of likely candidates in your town and state. You can locate prospects by using the Internet, checking local publications, and just asking around—use your network, other teachers, friends, neighbors, etc. (Check out the Web sites in Appendix B to assist you with locating wealthy individuals.) Once

31

you have compiled a list of possible donors, determine if one or more prospects have shown an interest in educational activities. Submit a letter of request and a copy of your proposal for consideration. Adhere to the same professional follow-up procedures as with any grant submitted to a foundation or corporation.

Funding-Search Strategies

The following strategies can help you stay focused during your funding search:

1. Look in your own backyard for funding; many foundations and corporations like to fund local programs/projects.

2. Do your homework; review the criteria of a potential funder very carefully before making contact or sending a proposal.

3. Contact the potential funder.

4. After you exhaust potential local funders, broaden your search to regional and national funders. Note: Many foundations and corporations do not limit their giving to local projects/programs.

5. Maintain a log or register that includes the results of your funding search, notes regarding the foundation or corporation, deadlines for proposal submission, conversations with funders, board of director meeting dates, and items that will help you remember key information. It is sometimes difficult to keep everything straight after making several contacts over a few weeks.

6. Review both Internet and print sources. Visit your local library; many have foundation and corporate directories available for your search.

These are just a few of the resources available to you as a grant seeker. The time you spend researching funding sources and reviewing grant-resource publications can greatly increase your chances of receiving funding for your educational project or program.

Chapter 4

Components of a Grant Proposal

DEVELOPING YOUR proposal is Step Six in the grant-writing process. Keep in mind a grant proposal is like a puzzle or a story. When all the pieces of a puzzle fit together, you see the whole picture. When the elements of a good story—plot, character development, problem/solution, setting, climax—come together, you catch the interest of the reader. Each component of a grant proposal has a job to do. If one component is lacking, then your reader (the funding officer or grant reviewer) will not see the entire puzzle or understand your story completely. This chapter provides a comprehensive overview of each component in a grant proposal.

Note: Funders (federal agencies, state and local governments, foundations, and corporations) do not always want or require all of the components discussed in this chapter. Sometimes the order of components required by a funder is different from those listed below. When you conduct your funding search and review the organization's guidelines, you will know which components are needed and the order in which they must be included. If the funder does not specify which components they want in the grant proposal, use the format described here.

Components of an Effective Grant Proposal

 Cover Letter
 Title Page
 Table of Contents
 Abstract (Executive Summary)
 Classroom/School/District Background
 Needs Statement
 Program/Project Description
  Goal(s)
  Objectives
  Project Activities
  Project Timeline
  Evaluation
  Budget
 Appendix

Cover Letter

For foundation and corporate proposals, not federal or state proposals, unless required in the guidelines.

The cover letter is the first component of a grant proposal. It should include a concise overview of your proposal, emphasizing the importance of, and need for, the program. The cover letter accompanies the written proposal but is not bound with it. Be creative, but do not exceed one-and-a-half pages.

Include a brief description of your organization as well as background information about your school district, school, or classroom. Mention why you chose to approach this particular funding agency. For example, you might state, "Based upon my research, your foundation appears to support the appropriate utilization of educational technology." Make a connection between your project and the funding agency's focus and areas of interest. Also state the amount of money you are requesting.

Send the cover letter to the attention of a specific individual. Remember the phone call you made earlier? Now is the time to utilize the information you gathered. All written communication should look very professional; print your cover letter on official letterhead, and never send a photocopy. If the funding source is located nearby, include a request to set up a meeting to discuss the details of your project or proposal.

I cannot overstate the importance of the cover letter. Many times it is your first contact with the funding agency. Spend considerable time reviewing the letter, rewriting it, and thinking about exactly what you want to say. Write the cover letter, put it aside for two or three days, and then go back and read it again. Ask yourself, "Would I be interested in funding this project after reading this letter?" Ask colleagues to read your letter, and listen to their feedback. Here is one sample of a cover letter (another example is included in Appendix E).

Sample Cover Letter

Dear Mr./Ms. _____ ,

As a teacher in the _____ County School System, I have conducted extensive research to locate companies that might be interested in helping me develop independent centers for my classroom that will address deficits in phonemic awareness, a building block of reading. Through my research, I have discovered that your company may be interested in assisting my efforts.

I am requesting a contribution of $1,500.00 for the total cost of supplies (and shipping/handling) to use in implementing independent learning centers that will focus on phonemic-awareness activities. These centers will be used by Special Education students in the Interrelated Resource Classroom to meet the phonemic-awareness goals and objectives stated in their Individual Education Plan during the 2008-2009 school year.

The total cost of this program is established at $1,500.00. The independent learning centers focusing on phonemic-awareness skills and basic reading will be used in my classroom during classroom time. I will serve as the project director of these centers. I have been an Interrelated Special Education teacher in _____ County for five years, and I am currently pursuing my Educational Specialist Certificate at _____ University.

I would greatly appreciate the opportunity to discuss this project with you at your convenience. I will contact you during the week of January 8, 2008, to discuss any potential interest on your part and perhaps arrange a meeting.

Sincerely,

Title Page

The title page should include a proposal title. Use a catchy or interesting title to capture the reader's interest. A funding officer or grant reviewer reads several grant proposals each week. A catchy title might help your proposal stand out. For example, three teachers developed a grant proposal and titled it "Project SPLASH," an acronym for Student-Powered Language and Study Habitat, which was designed to develop a language-immersion lab for needy students. The title caught the interest of the reader, and the funded grant enabled the teachers to purchase high-interest reading materials for their students.

The title page should also include the name of your school or school district, as well as the project director's name and position. The project director is the individual responsible for supervising the funded program. Include your address and phone number and the date on the title page. If you have a Web site, include the appropriate class, school, or district Web address. For example, a teacher writing a grant for his or her classroom should include the classroom's Web address; a proposal submitted for an entire school should include the school's Web site. District grants should list the district's Web site.

Sample Title Page

PROJECT: **D.A.T.A.**

(Distance-Accessed Technological Applications)

Submitted by:

Higher Expectations
601 Graystone Drive
Helpful, State 38901
(701) 855-0000
www.namegoeshere.org

Submitted to:

Foundation U.S.A.
[include address, etc?]
Project Director(s): C. Johns

Table of Contents

The table of contents indicates where each component is located in your grant proposal. Include a heading (I like boldface Courier New font in fourteen-point) for each major section of your proposal, along with the corresponding page number. List each appendix along with a brief description of the item in it. For example, "Appendix A: Letters of Support." Follow the funding source's guidelines. If they do not require a table of contents, don't include one.

Sample Table of Contents

TABLE OF CONTENTS

Abstract (Executive Summary)

The abstract gives the reviewer a good picture or description of the proposed project and explains the purpose and intended outcome(s) of the project. It should be clear, concise, and catchy. The abstract should be no longer than one page. If you have done a good job, after reading the abstract the reviewer will have a clear idea of the need for the project, how you will address the need, and the benefits that will be derived from it. The abstract should be written after the grant proposal has been developed. Consider this partial abstract from the Project SPLASH grant I mentioned earlier:

Sample Abstract

> When learning to swim, a person must be totally immersed in water. Likewise, when learning to become an effective user of language—a reader, writer, listener, and speaker—a child must be totally immersed in language. By providing a language-immersion lab, we will be helping our students dive into language and make a big splash.

The teachers who worked on this proposal spent days writing and rewriting the abstract. It was time well spent. They received the grant.

As with the cover letter, after you write your abstract, put it aside for two or three days, then go back and reread it. A common mistake I see in abstracts is a lack of clarity. You should not have to study the entire proposal to understand the abstract. Write the abstract as though it is the only description of your program that the funder will read. Be creative in developing this important grant component. Think of it this way: When someone (the funding office/grant reviewer) reads your abstract, will he want to fund your project? Does it say what you really want it to say? Have a colleague read your abstract. Is it clear? Is it concise? Does it catch the reader's interest? This is a very important part of your grant proposal. Spend appropriate time on your abstract and your cover letter. The payoff will be well worth your effort.

Background

The funding source needs to know about your organization. This is the place to inform them. Include background information about your classroom, school, school district, and community. Mention any relevant or unique features about your school or district.

If your school or district has been accredited by a national association, someone has already worked to develop background information for your school—feel free to use it. You may have to update it, but it could save you some time when developing this component. Do not be modest; mention exciting things that are happening in your classroom, school, and district. Based upon what you have learned about your potential funder, tailor what you write to align with the funder's focus and area of interest. I call this "tweaking." As you paint a picture of your class/school/ district, briefly introduce the identified need you plan to address. Do not go into great detail, though; you will do that in the next section of your grant proposal.

Sample Background

ABC Elementary School is located in the southern region of _____. Serving one of the fastest-growing areas of one of the fastest-growing cities in the state of _____, ABC Elementary has a continuously changing student population. With a current total of 728 students, 47 teachers, and two administrators, this elementary school has seen a lot of growth in its five years of life, due to the trend of Americans moving south. With only 10 percent of the school's population labeled as "economically disadvantaged" and another 10 percent of the school's population labeled as "students with disabilities," ABC Elementary appears to be a traditional school full of students who desire to succeed. The school, however, grosses the highest number of student referrals to the Support Team process and the highest number of referrals to Special Education testing in the district. This is a school full of students with the potential to succeed, given the right opportunity.

The school fares well academically, as do most schools in the County school system. It has met annual yearly progress standards each year, and the students perform consistently well on the ___ Test, actually gaining

1.05 percent in their ability to meet/succeed on _____ during the school year. It has even received the award for the highest percentage of students meeting and exceeding standards. This award, however, was given during a year when the school had minimal Special Education students with severe needs taking the end-of-year tests.

In upcoming years, the school may not fare as well academically. Based on eligibility, the students currently served in the Special Education department from grades 1 through 5 (the test years) have increased by 50 percent. However, the actual increase in students who intend to take the norm-referenced test is more important than the actual increase in numbers. The number of students who are eligible to receive services in Special Education under the Mild Intellectual Disability category has increased by100 percent, from zero students to three. The concern for any educator is how to reach the learning styles of these students, who tend to have half of the actual IQ of the average student. Creating and utilizing any and all resources, the teachers (100 percent are highly qualified at this school) have a tough road ahead of them. Implementing Project _____ will make it a bit less bumpy!

Needs Statement (Statement of Problem)

The needs statement establishes your need for a grant. In this section, you must show the funding source that you have a clear understanding of the problem or need you are going to address. Use supportive data, and provide any and all pertinent documentation.

Relevant documentation that indicates you have a need includes a needs assessment, which you can conduct in your own school or district. A needs assessment is an open-ended approach for gathering data; the questions included are usually broad in nature. For instance, a needs assessment might be sent out to all the parents in your school. One question might ask parents, "What is the greatest need you think the school has right now?" You will receive many different responses. Look for common themes. Let's say that 10 percent of the parents who respond indicate a perceived need for greater use of technology in the school. If you are writing a grant for technology, this information would help to document your need. You can administer a needs assessment to students, parents, or community members.

Statistical data gathered by your school or district can also be used in your needs statement. An example of this is pertinent testing data gathered on students. For instance, if 60 percent of your entire school population scored below grade level in reading on a nationally normed test, you would use this data to support a program focused on reading improvement.

Surveys are another good way to gather data on just about any need or problem. You can design your own survey and administer it to students, teachers, parents, and/or the community, depending on what you are attempting to document. Keep surveys brief; include just a few key questions. Name the survey appropriately. One team of teachers worked on a grant to incorporate more technology into their school curriculum. They developed a brief survey to administer to teachers in their school. It included ten questions and was simply called the "Teacher Technology Survey." One of the questions was, "Would you be willing to attend in-school professional development sessions to increase your knowledge of technology?" In their needs statement, these teachers were able to state that, according to the survey, 90 percent of the teaching faculty indicated they would attend professional development sessions aimed at increasing their knowledge of technology.

Another way to document a need is to conduct a brief literature review. Locate articles from journals that support your identified need or problem. Refer to the articles, and state how they support your need. Articles selected must seem like they were written solely to support your problem. If an article has only a passing connection to your need, do not use it; it will only confuse the reviewer. Three or four good articles will usually suffice.

Whenever possible, present data using a chart, table, or graph. A well-designed table or chart will convey important information to the funding source in a clear and powerful way. Using color in your charts, tables, and graphs is fine and can add to your proposal, but try not to go overboard.

Needs assessments, statistical data, surveys, and a good article can be included in the appendix of your grant. Remember, just stating that you have a need or problem is not enough. Funding sources like to see documentation so that they know you have done your homework.

Program/Project Description

In the previous section, you identified your need or problem, provided supporting data with several sources of documentation, and convinced the funder that you fully understand how the need should be addressed. Now you are going to describe how your specific project/program will address that need. This section of your proposal will include your project/program's goals, objectives, activities, timeline, evaluation plan, and budget.

The program/project description should show a direct relationship between identified needs and your project. State the expected benefits of your project, including who and how many people will be served. You must clearly explain how your project, program, or service is going to address the need. Begin with a clear overview of your program/project. Point out any creative or innovative aspects of how you are going to address the identified need. Many funders like to see innovative approaches to solving old problems.

Each component explained below provides the funding source with important information regarding your project/program. Every entry has its job to do and will help tell a complete story of your project and give the funding source a clear picture of what you intend to do. As you think about, then write, each of the sections, keep in mind how they complement each other.

Project/Program Goals—A goal is a general statement—usually one clearly written sentence—about what you want to accomplish with your program/project. Think about your project's end. What is your project's overall purpose? Your goals should explain to the grantor or funder what the project will achieve. A program/project can, of course, have more than one goal, and usually does.

Ask yourself this question: "If I accomplish these goals, will my identified need or problem be addressed?" Develop your goal statement based on the need or problem you discussed in your needs statement. Can you realistically accomplish your goals through the completion of your program/project? If not, rewrite your goals, because later, in the evaluation section of your grant, you will need to explain how you are going to evaluate your program's success. You will evaluate its success based upon whether or not you achieve the goals and objectives stated here.

Project/Program Objectives—Your objectives must be realistic, specific, and measurable. Keep them concise; list no more than eight to ten objectives per project/program. Fewer than eight objectives is also acceptable. Too many goals and objectives may suggest to the funding source that you are trying to accomplish more than you reasonably can with one grant. If possible, reduce the number, or collapse your goals and objectives. Sometimes you can merge two or three objectives into one while still maintaining the focus of what you are trying to achieve.

Your objectives must reflect your stated needs. For each objective, ask yourself, "If I accomplish this objective during the course of the program/project, will it address my stated goal?" The answer must be yes for each objective you write. If not, rewrite it so that the objective reflects a direct relationship to your goal.

Finally, review all of the objectives written for each goal. The number of objectives for each goal will vary. Most of my grants range from two to six objectives per goal, but this is just a guide; the project will determine your actual number of goals and objectives. As you review the objectives, ask yourself, "If my project/program accomplishes all of these objectives, will I meet my goal?" If your answer is yes, you are finished writing objectives for that goal. If the answer is no, you will need to add one or more objectives or rewrite the ones you have.

Your objectives will show the funding source how you will meet your goals. Carefully think about your project/program objectives because they will become the basis for your evaluation. As you write your program/project objectives, think about how you are going to evaluate each objective.

Program/Project Activities—This section describes how the procedures and activities of the project or program are to be implemented and conducted. Procedures and activities must be tied directly to your objectives and carefully explained to your reader. Briefly describe each activity that will be conducted during the project/program. Think about the "who, what, when, where, and how" of each activity and how it will help with your objectives.

Include a timeline for each activity in your grant proposal. Ask yourself, "Do my procedures and activities support my stated objectives?" The funding source wants to see a direct relationship between your stated needs, your program objectives, and your procedures and activities. Much of your budget will be spent on your program/project activities.

Timeline—I recommend including a timeline for the entire project or program in your proposal, indicating when activities and tasks will take place or be accomplished. A timeline can be day-by-day, week-by-week, or month-by-month, depending on your project/program. For a weeklong summer program to teach computer skills, include a day-by-day timeline of tasks and activities. A yearlong after-school reading program, on the other hand, would necessitate a month-to-month timeline of tasks and activities. A well-designed timeline will visually provide a greater understanding of your proposed project/program for the funding officer. Your school or district may have already purchased timeline software; social studies teachers sometimes have students use it to develop historical timelines. Check with your school/district's media specialist or technology person to see if this software is available.

Activities/Timeline
School Players 2008-2009

	Aug	Sep	Oct	Nov	Dec	Jan	Feb	Mar	Apr	May	June	July
Auditions	◎				◎							
	◎											
Distribute T-shirts	◎———		◎									
	◎				◎							
Dramatic Play					◎——			◎				
					◎————					◎		
Musical			◎						◎			
Dramatic Play							◎					
	◎————									◎		

44

Evaluation—Funding officers require that projects and programs be evaluated. The evaluation should be both *formative* and *summative* in nature. Formative evaluation is ongoing (during the program); summative evaluation occurs at the end of the program.

Evaluations will answer the following questions: Is the project/program accomplishing the stated goals and objectives? Were the activities successful? You must determine specific ways to show whether or not the program/project was successful. Its activities should also be evaluated. In this section of your proposal, explain how you plan to evaluate your program's goals, objectives, and activities even before your project is funded. Grant proposals often lose points on this component when reviewed by potential grantors, and many grants are not funded because the evaluation section is weak or nonexistent. You must clearly explain to the funding source how you will evaluate your program. Keep in mind that the evaluation process is easier when objectives are realistic, specific, and measurable.

Formative Evaluation—The table at the end of this section will help you with your formative evaluation. Create a separate table for each of your objectives. For example, if you have one goal and three objectives for that goal, you will have three tables. If you have three goals and each goal has three objectives, you will have nine tables.

At the top of each table, state the goal followed by its objectives. (You will usually have at least two objectives for each goal.) Remember: In the project/program activities section of your grant, you briefly described and listed each activity for your project/program. Go back and review that list, pulling out the activities that support the attainment of Objective #1. In the table under Project Activity, briefly state each activity. If you have two activities for Objective #1, you will complete two blocks under the Activity heading. In the block next to the activity description, state the desired outcome of that activity. An outcome is the desired result you want to achieve after conducting the activity. The assessment is how you will determine if you achieved that outcome. The outcome focuses on the results of your project/program.

Next, how will you assess an activity to determine if it was a success? State the activity in the Assessment block of the table. Next, under the Budget heading, include the total amount (do not break it down here) needed to conduct this activity. In the Timeframe block, indicate the day and month when this activity will take place. If you do not yet know the exact day, the month alone will do. Finally, who will be responsible to see that this activity takes place? Put that person's name (usually, but not always, the project director) in the last block.

As an example, let's use a grant designed to incorporate more technology into your school's curriculum. A technology survey was developed and administered to the teachers to document the need. The results of the survey indicated that 70 percent of the teachers want to learn how to use PowerPoint. Therefore, one of your activities might be to conduct a PowerPoint training session for those teachers. In the block under Project Activity you would write, "Conduct PowerPoint training for teachers." In the Desired Outcome block you could write, "Teachers will have a basic understanding of PowerPoint." In the Assessment block write, "Teachers will develop a four-slide presentation." Under the Budget block, write the total cost of the training session. Then include the date of the session and the name of the person planning the session in the appropriate blocks.

Again, complete a table for each project/program objective. If your proposal is limited to a certain number of pages, include the tables in an appendix. These tables will show the funding source that you have thought through the evaluation process, and they will give the funder detailed information about each activity.

Sample Formative Evaluation Table

Project Goal _____

Objective #1 _____

Project Activity	Desired Outcome	Assessment of Activity	Budget (cost of activity)	Timeframe	Responsible Person
#1					
#2					

Summative Evaluation—How will you determine the impact of your project/program? Did you accomplish your goals and objectives? Summative evaluation occurs at, or near, the end of the project. You will need to think about what data to gather in order to determine if you achieved your project/program's goals and objectives.

Sometimes projects/programs do not turn out as planned, and the goals and objectives are not met. Explain any circumstances or reasons for not accomplishing what you set out to do. Explain what you learned from the project/program that might be helpful in the future. This knowledge can be extremely valuable in meeting future needs and developing other grant proposals.

It is much easier to consider both your formative and summative evaluations if you think about how you will evaluate your accomplishments while you are planning your grant rather than after the project/program has ended. This is very important! Plan your evaluation from the beginning. This indicates to the funding source that you have thought out your project/program from the beginning to the end. Yes, you are developing a plan of evaluation for a project that has not been funded yet. This all goes back to your goals and objectives. Are they measurable? How will you measure success? What data will you need to gather to prove that you have met your goals and objectives? Your project/program will dictate the type of data you gather for evaluation purposes. Here are some examples for you to consider as you think about your summative evaluation:

- Pre- and post-test interest surveys (from students, parents, others)
- Pre- and post-test attitudinal inventories (of students, parents, etc.)
- Portfolio contents (can be used for both formative and summative evaluations)
- Teacher observations and anecdotal records (both formative and summative evaluations)
- Student observation/evaluation forms completed by facilitators (program personnel)
- Pre- and post-test inventories completed by participants
- Interviews of participants (can be formative and/or summative)

The evaluation section should include a narrative that describes how you will evaluate your grant project/program. Begin by stating that this project/program will be evaluated by both formative and summative techniques. The next paragraph should explain your plan for formative evaluation. Briefly explain how the table is set up, as discussed in the previous section. (Activities are assessed as they are conducted during the program.) The final paragraph will describe your summative evaluation techniques. Discuss what data will be gathered and how it will be analyzed to determine if you achieved/accomplished your goal(s) and objectives.

External Evaluation—There are times when external project/program evaluation is required. This means that an external evaluator—someone outside of your organization and not part of your program/project, who is knowledgeable about evaluation techniques—is one of the requirements in order to receive a grant. Very large federal or foundation grants may have this requirement. A good place to find an external evaluator is at a local college or university, where some faculty members will have a solid background in program evaluation and design. Look for someone who has worked as a program evaluator with education grants in the past; he or she can be a tremendous help in planning your project/program's evaluation design from the beginning. Usually, the grant will provide funds to pay for the external evaluation.

Even if you are not required to have an external evaluator, you may find it helpful to work with one. If you're having trouble with the evaluation-design section of your grant, check with a local college or university to see if a faculty member will help you. Many colleges and universities require faculty to provide service to schools as part of their job, and many education faculty members welcome the opportunity to work with a teacher, school, or district on a worthwhile project. However, for most grants you should be able to design the evaluation section of the grant yourself.

Budget—A budget is necessary to show how funds, equipment, or services will be used. The budget is directly related to the project objectives and activities. It explains to the funder how grant money will be spent during your project to accomplish your goals and objectives. Remember our table in the evaluation section? Your budget is a very important part of that. Funders have more questions about budgets, or how the money will be spent, than about any other grant component.

Based on your funding search, you will have a good idea of how much a funding source might provide. If a foundation awards an average-size grant of $30,000 and your project requires $25,000, you are in the ballpark. Asking for a little less than the source's average grant is a good strategy. Federal grants (RFPs) will state the amount that the agency will provide for a given project. For example, a federal agency may provide a grant for up to $250,000 for the integration of technology in schools. You might submit a proposal with a budget request of $225,250. This indicates to the funder that you took the time to calculate your budget.

Do not inflate your budget. Do your homework by calculating the actual cost of implementing your project/program. Sometimes this requires that you determine the cost of supplies, personnel, equipment, etc., as you prepare your budget. You will need to determine all the costs associated with your project/program. You cannot go back to the funding source after your grant is funded and ask for more money. To do so is seen as poor planning on your part.

Some funders have their own format for budget preparation. In this case, use their format to prepare your budget. Many times this simply requires plugging in your estimated costs using their budget format. More often than not, the funder does not have a specific format, in which case you will create your own budget.

Basic Budget Terms

- **Direct Costs**, also called line items, are the expenses necessary to carry out the program/project: salaries and wages, employee benefits, travel, equipment purchase or lease, materials and supplies, consultants' fees, etc.

- **Indirect Costs** (overhead) are indirect expenses such as utilities, janitorial services, rental fees, administrative costs, maintenance, and telephone usage. Indirect costs are usually a percentage of total direct costs. In their application package, funding agencies will state the percentage of indirect costs allowed.

- **Matching Funds** can be either "hard" money or "soft" (in-kind) money. A "hard money" match requirement means a dollar-for-dollar match. For example, if you request $25,000 from a funder, you will be required to match that amount with $25,000 of your organization's funds. A "soft money" or in-kind match is a non-cash contribution from your organization to the program/ project, such as use of current personnel for the project/program without payment from the grant, use of the facility to house the project/program, use of existing equipment not purchased through the grant, or items that would be classified as indirect costs if indirect costs are not requested in the grant.

- A **Budget Narrative** shows the funder how you came up with each line-item cost (see Example 2 on page XX). Some funders do not require a budget narrative as part of the grant proposal, but you should still include one.

Provide as much detail in your budget as needed to clearly show how the funds will be expended. *Remember:* All items in the program/project budget and the budget narrative must be clearly delineated in your project/program description. *The budget supports your program goals, objectives, and activities.*

Sample Budgets

Example 1: Line-Item Budget

Line Item	Grant Funds Requested	Matching Funds
1. PERSONNEL	$30,500	
2. EMPLOYEE BENEFITS	$6,100	
3. TRAVEL	$3,000	$1,000
4. EQUIPMENT	$3,600	$7,200
5. SUPPLIES	$700	
6. CONSULTANTS	$2,500	
7. INSTRUCTIONAL MATERIALS	$8,000	
8. CURRICULUM MATERIALS	$4,000	$4,500
9. Other line items as needed for your project/program	_____	
Matching Funds	$12,700	
Total funds requested	$58,400	

Keep in mind:

- Budget line items and direct costs vary from grant to grant depending on the needs of your project/program.

- Matching funds are not required by most funders. However, if you can show a substantial match, even if it is not required for the grant (and the funder does not specifically state not to include a match), go ahead and show your financial commitment to the project/program.

- A budget narrative will follow your line-item budget and explain/break down the dollar amount listed on each budget line (Items 1–8). For example, in Line 2 the amount of $6,100 is listed. In the budget narrative you would explain how you came up with that amount: The project director's part-time salary times 20 percent for benefits such as insurance ($30,500 X 20% = $6,100). Note that this 20 percent figure was obtained by calling the district's human resources office.

Example 2: Program Budget with Narrative

The following budget was taken from a teacher-developed grant to expand a high school theatre program. Even though a match was not required by the funding agency, the teacher wanted to show that the school and students were committed enough to the program to come up with $3,000 on their own. The budget narrative follows the program budget and provides the funder with a breakdown of each budget item.

Program Budget

Line	Budget Item	Grant Funds Requested	Matching Funds
A	Club T-Shirts	$640	0
B	Jr. Thespian Dues	$490	0
C	High School Theater Tickets	$385	0
D	Theater Tickets	$1,500	$1,000
E	Costumes	$1,500	$1,000
F	Sets/Props	$1,500	$1,000
G	Promotions/Marketing	$1,000	0
H	Teacher Stipends	$2,000	0
I	**Total amount requested**	**$9,015**	**$3,000**

Budget Narrative

A. Club T-shirts will be purchased for all participants in the Players group. The T-shirts will be worn to promote the program and create camaraderie within the group. (64 students X $10 = $640)

B. The Educational Theatre Association promotes and strengthens school theater programs through the International Thespian Society. Students in middle school can join the Junior Thespian Society. Students' membership points from middle school will be added to those they earn by participating in their high school thespian society.

C. Students in the Players group will attend the high school's fall theater production. The middle school is our feeder school, and this will give the students an opportunity to make comparisons between a high school and a middle school production. (64 students X $6 = $385)

D. The _____ Theatre is a professional theater company in _____. The students will be exposed to a professional production and talk to artists who have chosen acting as a career. (50 X $30 = $1,500)

E. Costumes will be created and purchased for four performances. These costumes will be stored in our theater closet and used again in future productions.

F. Sets and props will be created and purchased for four performances. These sets and props will be stored in our theater closet for use in future productions.

G. Promotions and marketing will include tickets, playbills, posters, newspaper ads, and photos.

H. Four teachers will sponsor and direct this program. These teachers will each receive a $500 yearly stipend.

Example 3: Project Budget

This budget was taken from a project created to provide enrichment opportunities for youth in an underserved community. The explanation section was added to further clarify each line item. Notice the use of volunteers in this grant project. Volunteers can help reduce the cost of a project, and sometimes their time can be counted as an in-kind match, if needed.

Project Budget

Categories	Item	Quantity	Cost/unit	Totals	Explanation
Administrative/ Training	30 hours (volunteer training)	5 people	$15.00 per hour	$2,250.00	The training will familiarize potential tutors with administrative procedures, pedagogical techniques, and ethical considerations. (30 hrs. X 5 people X $15.00/hr. = $2,250.00)
	Printing			$2,000.00	Quarterly newsletter and letterhead
	Postage	500 per quarter	$.35	$700.00	Postage costs for newsletters 500 X $.35 X 4 quarters = $700.00
Academic Tutorial	Laptops	3	$1,300.00	$3,900.00	Laptops are required for students to complete classroom assignments (problem solving/ critical thinking) and to perform research on the Internet. It is critical, due to security, that the computers are mobile.
	Portable printers	2	$200.00	$400.00	Printers are required for students to complete classroom assignments and to perform research on the Internet. It is critical, due to security, that the printers are mobile.
	Network router	1	$150.00	$150.00	A network router will enable students to have access to the printers and to the school's Internet, with the advantage of allowing the laptops and printers to remain wireless.
	PCMIA "WIFI" cards for the 3 laptops	3	$80.00	$240.00	"WIFI" cards will enable students to have access to the printers and to the school's Internet, with the advantage of allowing the laptops and printers to remain wireless.

Categories	Item	Quantity	Cost/unit	Totals	Explanation
Academic Software	Kids Lit	1	$1,500.00	$1,500.00	Literacy-based reading program designed specifically for after-school programs
Personnel	Salary for site coordinator	1 person	$30,000.00	$30,000.00	The site coordinator will be responsible for coordinating all services offered by ____.
	Monthly stipend for 3-person leadership team members	9 months	$300.00	$2,700.00	This team will assist the co-director and class leaders in administrative duties. The leadership team is paid a modest stipend of $100.00 per month for their efforts beyond their initial duties as volunteers.
	Pay for 2 class leaders per week (includes tutoring, enrichment activities, and classroom visits)	40 weeks	$15.00 per hour	$6,000.00	The class leaders will be responsible for 5 tutors, who will work with the class of 10 students. The class leaders will visit the classroom each week and consult with teachers on the ongoing performance of each child in their class. Class leaders will be paid $15 per hour.(2 X 40 X 5 (hours) X $15.00 = $6,000)
	External Program Evaluator	1	$2,400.00	$2,400.00	Qualitative observational and interview assessment with an independent evaluator.
Social Discovery Activities	Admission or registration fees for 30 students	40 weeks	$100.00	$4,000.00	Enrichment activities will be designed to improve and broaden students' awareness of culture and to train them in essential life skills. The ultimate aim of the enrichment program is to increase the motivation for lifelong learning and to improve student behavior in school.
	Bussing for enrichment activities	During program 40 weeks	$40.00	$1,600.00	Students and staff will be transported to and from enrichment activities via a reserved school bus.
End-of-Year Banquet	100 people associated with project	1	$2,500.00	$2,500.00	Students and volunteers will be recognized for outstanding work.
Summer Program	Camp fees	12	$250 each student	$3,000.00	Admissions fees for summer camps.
	Transportation costs	12	$250 for bus rental	$3,000.00	Bus rental cost for transporting students.
Total funds requested				$66,340.00	

Example 4: Multi-Year Budget

The following budget was taken from a multiyear federal grant project. Notice the direct and indirect costs listed for each year. This grant had a matching requirement (in-kind/soft money). Next to the direct cost is the non-federal contribution from the requesting organization. In Year 1, the total direct cost requested from the federal program was $281,992 and the match from the organization was $399,949. Indirect costs could not exceed 8 percent (federal stipulation) of total direct costs ($281,992 × .08 = $22,559). The budget narrative, providing a detailed explanation of each direct-cost category, would follow this form. (Direct costs are Lines 1–7 of the budget.)

Direct Costs	1st Year Federal	1st Year Non-Federal	2nd Year Federal	2nd Year Non-Federal	3rd Year Federal	3rd Year Non-Federal	4th Year Federal	4th Year Non-Federal
1. Salaries & Wages	66,000	166,537	66,000	163,437	66,000	163,537	198,000	493,511
2. Employee Benefits	17,992	11,512	17,992	11,512	17,992	11,512	53,976	34,536
3. Travel	10,200	16,000	13,350	17,000	13,350	18,000	36,900	51,000
4. Equipment	6,000	156,750	5,200	88,750	-------	88,750	11,200	334,250
5. Materials & Supplies	5,000	18,900	5,000	10,900	5,000	10,900	15,000	40,700
6. Consultants	43,500	23,700	38,500	13,500	35,500	13,000	117,500	50,200
7. Other (Rental Fees)	133,300	6,550	94,300	6,550	76,300	6,850	303,600	19,950
A. Total Direct Costs: 1-7	281,992	399,949	240,342	311,649	214,142	312,549	736,476	1,024,147
B. Indirect Costs (not to exceed 8% of total direct costs)	22,559	31,996	19,227	24,938	17,131	25,004	58,918	81,938
C. Total Costs (A + B)	304,551	431,945	259,569	336,587	231,273	337,553	795,394	1,106,085
D. Total Program Cost (Federal & Non-Federal)	736,496		596,156		568,826		1,901,478	

Appendix—The final component of an effective grant proposal is the appendix. Items that support your proposal but do not necessarily fit in any other place should be included in this section. All items in the appendix should stand alone and need no further explanation. A few examples of what might be included in the appendix are:

- *Project director's résumé:* It's important for the funding officers to know a little bit about the project director. Other key individuals on the project should also have a résumé included in the appendix.

- *Statement of Assurances:* Sometimes required, especially for federal grants; it is a statement signed by you indicating that you will not violate any civil or human rights during your program/project. Your local board of education has probably approved such a statement. It will be available from your principal or human resources office.

- *Letters of endorsement:* This is a very important part of your proposal. Include four to six letters written by significant individuals in your school, school district, and community who have reviewed your grant proposal. The letters should show that you have identified a true need and that the writers believe your proposal will address that need. Depending on the focus of your grant, you might want to obtain letters of support from your school administration, other teachers, the PTA/PTO president, an associate superintendent, a superintendent, a board member, or appropriate community leaders. Occasionally, you might be asked to write the letter of support yourself, and the reference will place it on their own stationery. If so, make sure each letter reads differently.

- *Charts or graphs:* If you have a chart or graph that stands alone, and it supports your proposal, include it in the appendix.

- *Journal articles:* If you have one or two journal articles that strongly support your proposal, you may want to include them.

Sample Letter of Support

> As the principal of _____ Elementary School, I can assure you that our school is filled with dedicated and hardworking teachers who care about our students, their families, and the community as a whole. We, as a staff, work hard to recognize and celebrate our students' cultures, while at the same time striving to acclimate our students to American culture and teach them the skills necessary to be successful.
>
> For the 2007–2008 school year, our school did not make Annual Yearly Progress (AYP). This means that our school community did not meet all of the necessary benchmarks set by the Federal No Child Left Behind Law as stated by the government. This was a first for our school, and it has led our staff to refocus on providing additional support for those students who have the greatest need.
>
> Our school has become increasingly filled with immigrant families, predominantly from Spanish-speaking countries; 61 percent of last year's students were Hispanic. This portion of our population seems to have the greatest need for additional support in the areas of reading and writing the English language.
>
> One of our greatest challenges has been to help our Spanish-speaking students read, write, and speak English at a high level. In order to achieve this goal, I would support and encourage funding for a Saturday School program to include our fourth- and fifth-grade students, specifically focusing on those with the greatest need for English-language acquisition.
>
> Sincerely,

During the past twenty-five years, grant writing has become more competitive. A well-developed proposal is essential to your success. Funders want to feel assured that their contributions will make a difference in the lives of children. A first-class proposal goes a long way in assuring a grantor of your program or project's worthiness.

The fourteen components discussed in this chapter are widely utilized in educational grant proposals. Their order and combination will vary based on the requirements of the funder. It is critical to carefully review the funder's guidelines (when conducting a funding search) before preparing your grant proposal.

By tailoring your proposal to meet the funder's criteria, you will greatly increase the chances of receiving funding for your project or program. If a funder does not give specific guidelines about the components of a proposal, follow the format discussed in this chapter. As you can see, each component of a grant proposal has a job to do. When a grant proposal is properly composed, each component provides key information to the funder about your program or project. What is—or is not—in your grant proposal can make the difference between getting funded and getting rejected.

Chapter 5

Evaluating Grant Proposals

IT IS helpful for grant writers to understand how funding sources evaluate grant proposals. If you have an idea of what funders are looking for, you can make sure to address those yardsticks in your proposal. Of course, there are so many foundations, corporations, federal agencies, wealthy individuals, and state and local officials, not all funders look for the same things. However, the following guidelines will help your proposal stand out—in a good way.

What do funders look for when they evaluate grant proposals?

Funders want to see that your grant proposal accomplishes the following:

- Identifies a true need.
- Demonstrates a clear understanding of the need.
- Indicates a clear plan for meeting the need.
- Shows that the needs, objectives, procedures, activities, and evaluation are all realistic and in sync.
- Has a realistic budget.
- Illustrates the capability of the project director.
- Indicates that project personnel have credibility/ability.

- Shows how the project/program is a corporate or foundation priority.
- Addresses all funding-agency criteria.
- Explains the suitability of the facilities.
- Includes appropriate evaluation procedures.

Funders look to see that you have identified a true need, that your proposal demonstrates a clear understanding of that problem or need, and that you have developed an idea that will address that need. The proposal must also indicate a clear plan for solving or meeting that need. Your needs, objectives, procedures, activities, and evaluation plan must all be realistic and in sync. Funders look to see if your objectives address a true need and are specific, concise, realistic, and measurable.

The funders are going to evaluate your proposal based on your budget requests, so give especially careful thought to the budget. All items in the program/project budget and the budget narrative must be clearly delineated in your project/program description. The budget must support your program/project goals, objectives, and activities.

Funders will look at the capability of the program/project director and the credibility of the project personnel. Do not let this concern you too much. As teachers and administrators, you have considerable ability; you have been well trained to address student needs.

It is important that you match your program/project with the funding priority of the foundation, corporation, or federal agency to which you submit your proposal. Make sure your program meets the guidelines of the funding organization. Again, your proposal must address all the funding agency's criteria. Tailor your proposal to that particular funding agency, and make sure you follow their criteria to the letter.

Funders want to see that you have a suitable facility for your project or program (in most cases this will be a school facility). They will also look at your evaluation procedures to ensure that they are appropriate.

Using the Grant Proposal Rubric

I have developed a rubric for reviewing a grant proposal before it is submitted to a funding source. Take a moment to review the grant rubric in Appendix F. Then rate the foundation proposal in Appendix E by using the rubric. Tally your score and compare it with my evaluation, which is located in Appendix F.

Use the grant-writing rubric to evaluate your grant proposals prior to submission. If you are not happy with your score, think about how you can improve your proposal. The rubric will become second nature to you, and after a while, you won't even need it.

Grant-Proposal Tips

Gain Approval. Remember that teacher who did not get the approval of her administrator before submitting a grant proposal? She then failed to get approval for her grant. Don't let that happen to you. Make sure you get appropriate support and approval for your project at the beginning of the process.

Reread Before Submitting. After you complete your proposal, put it aside for a few days, then go back and reread it to make sure it says what you want it to say. Have another person proofread your proposal for spelling errors or mistakes.

Look Professional. Make sure your proposal looks as professional as possible. Have it professionally bound at your local copy center (I like the spiral binding), and never send a copy. Purchase high-quality paper for your proposals.

Make a Good First Impression. Spend extra time on your cover sheet and abstract. The wording of your proposal should flow smoothly and be easy to understand.

Stay Away From Jargon. Funding officers have told me that they like a proposal that's direct, straightforward, and uses little education jargon. If you use any terms in your proposal, define them immediately.

Use a Team Approach. When developing your proposal, it is rewarding to work with a team of motivated educators who want to address the needs of their students. However, for consistency of format and wording, only one person should actually write the grant proposal.

Write About What You Know. As educators, we know a great deal about children and their needs. This is where we should spend our time when developing proposals. It is obvious to a funding officer if the grant writer lacks expertise in a particular area.

Keep It Short. For most foundation and corporate grants, keep the length of your proposal to under twelve pages, excluding the appendix. Federal grants are usually more involved than foundation or corporate grants and, thus, will be longer.

Be Selective. Determine which funding agency is most likely to be interested in your project or program. Do your homework on the foundation or corporation before approaching them with your proposal, and make sure they fund similar projects. Sending your proposal to the wrong organization is a waste of time for both you and them.

Plan Your Budget Carefully. Check the typical dollar amount of grants made by the organization you are submitting your proposal to. If the foundation's typical grant is $25,000, don't ask for $30,000. Never inflate your budget.

Develop a Catchy Title. A great title can catch the eye of a funder and set your grant apart from the dozens of others he or she will read that week.

Get a Critique. Ask someone not involved with your project to critique your proposal before submission. Sometimes we get very close to our work and are not as objective as we should be.

Obtain Letters of Support. I suggest you include at least four to six letters of support in your appendix.

Follow Agency Guidelines. It is vitally important that your proposal follows the guidelines of the funding agency. If the funder's guidelines don't include all the components we have discussed, or they want them in a different order, follow their guidelines.

More Quick Tips

- Build relationships with funding agencies.
- Provide recognition for the funding agency that awards you a grant.
- Effectively manage your grant by keeping detailed records of expenditures.
- Spend the money exactly as you stated in the grant.
- Contact the funding agency if you have questions about a grant program.
- Hand-deliver your proposal, if the funder is located near you.
- Look in your own backyard for funding. Many businesses and organizations prefer to give grants locally.
- Do your homework; find out which foundations or corporations might be interested in your project/program.
- Continue to increase your knowledge by keeping track of new potential funding sources.
- Submit your proposal *before* the deadline.
- Begin a file on grant writing; include proposals, books, articles, and funding sources.
- *Don't give up!* Stubbornness is a good trait in a grant writer.

Chapter 6

Small-Grant Acquisition

THE PROCEDURES in small-grant acquisition differ in several ways from those for obtaining large grants. Small grants usually require much less time and effort than large grants. Also, potential funders are usually local. Finally, the grant proposal is much less important than with large grants. In fact, a grant proposal is usually not necessary in order to acquire a small grant. In most cases, a letter of request will suffice.

Remember, a grant is more than just money. We defined a grant as any goods, services, or funds provided. So if someone donated time to set up a social studies fair or has provided your class with a set of maps, you have already received a small grant. Congratulations!

How to Acquire a Small Grant

Let's lift the veil of mystery and look at the steps for small-grant acquisition.

Develop a Fundable Idea. Ask yourself the following questions: Do my students have a need that should be addressed? How can this be done? Remember that a need exists when there is a difference between what is and what could be. A good place to start is to discuss your idea with colleagues and parents. Once you think you have a worthwhile idea, it's important to present it to school administrators for their approval and support before you proceed any further.

Cultivate Contacts in Your Own Backyard. Do your research by gathering data about possible funding sources. Think about your community. Which organizations or businesses might be interested in your idea? Make a list of places to contact, such as civic clubs, professional groups, and local businesses—even individuals. Drop by and welcome new businesses to the area; introduce yourself and mention your project. Ask if they might be interested in assisting with your efforts. They may be eager to establish themselves in the community by supporting an educational endeavor.

Develop a Relationship. Personal contact with a potential funder is critical in small-grant acquisition. If you don't know the grantor personally, perhaps you have a mutual acquaintance who would be willing to arrange an introduction. If not, you will need to call and introduce yourself. Begin by explaining your reason for contacting that person or company, and request a meeting to discuss your project.

Explain Your Need. At the meeting, be prepared to clearly explain both your project and the assistance that you are requesting. The person you speak with may or may not need a few days to think over your idea or get approval. In any case, send a note thanking the person for talking with you. Whether or not you receive the grant, be appreciative of the person for their time and interest. If your grant does get approved, prepare a letter of request for the funding source. This should include a brief overview of your project/idea; more often than not, it will take the place of a formal grant proposal. Even though a letter of request is not as important as personal contact with the funding source, it reflects your professional approach to grant solicitation.

Express Your Gratitude. Even for small grants, be sure to provide recognition for the funding source. Here are a few suggestions for how to do this:

- Take a photo of the goods, services, or funds donated and send it to the funder with a note of appreciation.

- Write a brief article and submit it to your local newspaper. Sometimes a reporter will do this for you, but if not, you can take the initiative.

- Ask the contributor to visit the school and observe first-hand how your project/idea is helping kids. Provide him or her with recognition during the visit.

- In addition to your own letter of thanks, have students write thank-you notes as well.

Small-grant acquisition can be fun and beneficial. It does require some effort, but the rewards for you and your students (and your school and your community) will be well worth it. In addition, your colleagues may look at you a little differently once you've received a grant! Don't be surprised if other teachers seek out your expertise for their own grant projects.

Sample Letter of Request

Dear (Donor),

    I appreciate you taking the time to talk with me a few days ago.

    As you may recall, I am a seventh-grade social studies teacher at _____ Middle School. This year I have been researching computer simulations as a unique and interesting way to develop problem-solving skills in my students.

    Recently, I learned of an exceptional computer-simulation program that helps students use problem-solving techniques to make environmentally sound decisions. It examines how individual decisions can have far-reaching effects on the environment; the decisions of people in the past have had an important effect on our lives today, just as our actions will certainly affect future generations. That's why it is so important to teach students how to make good decisions.

    In a few weeks, I will be teaching an interdisciplinary unit on the environment, and I would like to integrate this computer-simulation program into the unit. My principal, Ms. Smith, also thinks this would be a good way to interest students and stimulate problem-solving skills.

    You are probably aware that due to cuts in the state budget, our funding has been reduced by 20 percent. Unfortunately, most of my classroom budget is spent buying necessities (textbooks, maps, etc.) and maintaining equipment needed in the classroom.

Your company has a reputation for supporting worthwhile educational projects in our community. The cost of the computer-simulation program, which can be used many times, is $325. Any contribution you can make will bring significant benefits to our students. Your consideration is appreciated, and I welcome the opportunity to answer any questions you may have. Please call me at the school, at XXX-XXXX.

Sincerely,

Time to Try It Yourself

Tight budgets mean that as educators you must look for outside funds to meet the many needs of your students. Grant funds can help you develop worthwhile programs and projects to meet those needs. You can become an excellent grant writer; outside funding for both large and small grants is available if you take the time to look. Sometimes it might take only a few hundred dollars to address a need in your classroom. Become familiar with the grant-writing resources discussed in this book. Develop your skill at using these resources to locate potential funders. Always keep in mind the critical necessity of matching your program or project with the funding source's area of interest, then develop a strong grant proposal that supports your program/project. Utilize the grant-writing rubric to help you develop grant proposals until you are confident with the various components. I suggest you continue to increase your knowledge of grant writing by beginning a grant-writing file to house articles and books on grant writing, sample grants you run across, possible funding sources, and Internet sites.

Grant writing can be fun and beneficial. It does require some time and effort, but the tremendous satisfaction of knowing that your students are benefiting from your hard work is personally and professionally rewarding. Good luck, and best wishes with your grant-writing efforts.

Appendix A

Glossary of Grant-Writing Terms

Applicant: Individual or organization seeking a grant.

Application for Federal Education Assistance: The grant application form used by the Department of Education.

Application Notice: Published in the Federal Register; invites applications for discretionary grants.

Application Package: A package that contains the application notice for one or more programs and all the information and forms needed to apply for a discretionary grant.

Appropriation: The amount of funds authorized by Congress allowing federal agencies to make awards under legislated programs.

Authorization: Congressional legislation establishing a specific program.

Assurances: Requirements that applicants agree to observe as a condition of receiving federal funding.

Authorizing Legislation: A law passed by Congress that establishes or continues a grant program.

Award: A grant.

Awarding Agency: Funding agency that gives a grant.

Award Notice: Formal written notification from a funding agency to a grantee, stating that a grant has been awarded.

Block Grant: A grant from a government funding source made on the basis of some formula to a number of different recipients.

Boilerplate: Parts of a proposal that may include assurances, a cover sheet, and background information.

Budget: Estimated cost of conducting the proposed project, consisting of direct and indirect costs, matching costs (if any), and a budget narrative.

Budget Narrative: Explains in sufficient detail how the grantee came up with each line-item cost in the budget.

Budget Period: Span of time into which a project period is divided for budgetary purposes; usually twelve months.

Construction Grant: Grant limited to constructing or remodeling a physical facility.

Catalog of Federal Domestic Assistance (CFDA): Publication that lists the funding programs of all federal agencies and gives information about a program's authorization, fiscal details, accomplishments, regulations, guidelines, eligibility requirements, information contacts, and application and award process.

CFDA Number: Identifying number for a federal program.

Competitive Review Process: The process used to select discretionary grants for funding. Experts score applications, and the most highly scored applications are considered for funding.

Continuation Award: Additional funding awarded to the same grant for a budget period following the initial budget period of a multiyear discretionary grant.

Corporation: An entity formed and authorized by the state to act as an individual (i.e., to own, buy, and sell property; to enter into contracts, etc.) with the right of succession and to issue shares of stock, which represent shares of ownership of the corporation.

Cover Letter: Introductory letter that provides a concise overview of a grant proposal.

Deadline Date: The date by which an applicant must submit an application in order for it to be considered for funding.

Demonstration Grant: Grant made to support the demonstration and testing of the feasibility or piloting of a particular approach to service delivery, research, training, or technical assistance.

Direct Costs: Expenses directly associated with carrying out the sponsored project.

Discretionary Grant: An award of financial assistance in the form of money by the federal government to an eligible grantee, usually made on the basis of a competitive review process.

e-Grants: A term for the Department of Education's electronic grants initiative, which allows applicants and grantees to do business with the Department over the Internet.

e-Reports: The Department of Education's electronic reporting system, which makes it possible for grantees to submit their annual grant performance reports via the Internet.

External Evaluation: A project or program evaluation conducted by someone not involved in the program/project who is knowledgeable about evaluation techniques.

Federal Register: A daily notice of federal proposed and final regulations, legal notices, presidential proclamations and executive orders, federal agency documents having general applicability and legal effect, documents required to be published by an act of Congress, and other federal agency documents of public interest. The Register is prepared by the National Archives and Records Administration for public distribution by the Government Printing Office.

Field Reader (Reviewer): An individual who serves the Department of Education by reviewing and evaluating proposals.

Formative Evaluation: The ongoing evaluation of a project or program during the implementation period.

Foundation: A nonprofit, non-governmental organization that assists other nonprofit organizations in the practice of providing grants.

Formula Grant: A grant that the Department of Education is directed by Congress to make to grantees, the amount of which is established by a formula based on certain criteria that are written into the legislation and program regulations.

Funding Officer: Someone who reviews grant proposals and makes funding recommendations.

Funding Priorities: A way of focusing a competition on the areas in which the funding source is particularly interested in receiving applications. Funding Source (Funder): The source of a grant; can be a corporation, foundation, business, federal or state agency, or an individual.

Funding Search: The action of identifying a funder for a specific program or project.

501(c)(3): The tax designation provided to tax-exempt organizations by the Internal Revenue Service.

Grant: An award of funds, services, or materials.

Grant Award Notification (GAN): Official document signed by a program official who is authorized to obligate the Department of Education in financial matters. The GAN states the amount and the terms and conditions of an award for a discretionary grant or cooperative agreement.

Grantee: The individual or organization receiving a grant who is responsible or accountable for it.

Grantor: The federal or state agency, foundation, corporation, nonprofit organization, or individual who awards a grant to a recipient.

Grant-Writing Process: A systematic procedure for obtaining grants for worthwhile educational projects and programs. Differs among funders but generally includes identifying a need, obtaining documentation, acquiring support and approval from school administrators, conducting a funding search, contacting the funding source, developing a grant proposal, submitting the proposal, and following up.

Grant-Writing Team: A group of educators working together on a grant proposal to capitalize on the knowledge and experience of each group member.

Guidelines: Specific criteria used to evaluate a proposal. A funder's criteria spell out the requirements that the proposal must address with respect to its components and format.

Indirect Costs: The expenses indirectly associated with the sponsored project, including administrative expenses, utilities, physical plant maintenance, library facilities, etc. They are usually expressed as a percentage of the total direct costs. Rates are sometimes negotiable between the applicant and the funding agency.

Indirect Cost Rate Agreement: A formalized, written, and signed agreement between a recipient and a federal agency that specifies the treatment of indirect costs. The agreement includes, at a minimum, the approved rate(s); base(s) to which the rate(s) apply; applicable fiscal year; specific treatment of certain items of cost; general terms and conditions; and any special remarks. The rates and cost treatment laid out in the agreement are accepted and used by all federal agencies unless prohibited or limited by statute.

Indirect Cost Rate: A percentage established by a federal department or agency for a grantee organization, which the grantee uses in computing the dollar amount it charges to the grant to reimburse itself for the indirect costs of a grant project.

In-Kind Contribution: Non-cash contribution to a project or program by the grantee. Such a contribution usually consists of volunteer personnel, equipment, supplies, and/or rent that directly supports the program or project.

Letter of Intent: A letter sent by a grantee to a funding source stating his or her intention to submit a grant proposal.

Letter of Inquiry: A letter sent by a grantee to a funding source that contains a brief description or overview of a proposed project or program to see if the funding source is interested in funding the project.

Letter of Request: Used for small-grant acquisition. This brief overview of the project or program for which the grantee is requesting a grant usually takes the place of a formal grant proposal.

Letter of Support: A letter written by a significant individual in the grantee's school, school district, or community supporting the proposed project/program.

Local Government: Level of government below the state level, including counties, cities, and towns.

Matching Funds: Participation by the grantee in the cost of a program on a dollar-for-dollar basis or other predetermined ratio.

Multiyear Grants: Grants that are funded for more than one year (usually federal grants).

Notice of Grant Award: Formal written notice from the grantor that specifies the amount of the grant, its time period, and any special requirements.

990-PF: A document that foundations must submit to the Internal Revenue Service. Provides grant seekers with valuable information about a foundation.

Performance Report: A report about the specific activities that the recipient of a discretionary grant or cooperative agreement has performed during the budget or project period.

Planning Grant: Grant intended to support activities necessary to design and plan a particular program or project, to design and plan programs in a particular geographic area and/or a particular field of service, or to engage in inter-agency planning and coordination. Planning grants often include research, study, coordination, community participation, community organization, and education activities as components of the planning activities.

Program Staff: A group of staff members in a program office responsible for all phases of the grants process including the review, award, administration, and closeout of discretionary grants.

Program Regulations: Regulations that implement legislation passed by Congress to authorize a specific grant program. They generally include applicant and participant eligibility criteria, nature of activities funded, allowability of certain costs, selection criteria under which applications will be selected for funding, and other relevant information.

Project Period: The total amount of time for which a federal agency promises to fund a grant and authorizes a grantee to implement the project described in the application. A multiyear award obligates funds for the first twelve months and, if certain conditions are met, for subsequent budget periods.

Project Director (Principal Investigator): The individual responsible for the funded project who makes sure the project is implemented as stated in the grant proposal. The project director is the contact person for the funding source but does not have to be the same person who wrote the grant. A school may establish a grant-writing team that develops various grant proposals to meet school needs. The project director could be someone who is not on the team but who will oversee the project if it is funded.

Proposal: Formal written document that provides detailed information to a funder about the proposed implementation and cost of a specific program or project.

Request for Proposal (RFP): An invitation, detailing project requirements, issued by a funding agency in response to which applicants may submit a grant proposal.

Research Grant: Grant to support research in the form of studies, surveys, evaluations, investigations, and experimentation.

Seed Money: Funds made available for pilot projects in preparation for application for external funding.

Site Visit: Onsite visit from the funding source to the site of the project or program to evaluative its performance.

Solicited Proposal: A request for a written grant proposal from a funding source.

Summative Evaluation: Occurs at, or near, the end of a project or program.

Sustainability: The capability of a program/project to continue after its grant funding ends.

Unsolicited Proposal: A written proposal submitted to a funding agency without the grantor's request for it.

Appendix B

Grant-Writing Resources

Grants and Funding Web Sites

www.cof.org
Council on Foundations focuses on international philanthropy.

www.cfda.gov
The Catalog of Federal Domestic Assistance provides access to a database of all federal programs available to state and local governments (including the District of Columbia); federally recognized Indian tribal governments; territories (and possessions) of the United States; domestic public, quasi-public, and private profit and nonprofit organizations and institutions; specialized groups; and individuals.

Search this database to find assistance programs that meet your requirements and for which you are eligible. Then contact the office that administers the program and find out how to apply.

www.dhhs.gov
The U S. Department of Health and Human Services has many grant opportunities.

www.ed.gov
A primary prospective funding source for educators. The U.S. Department of Education's Web site provides a wealth of information for organizations interested in educational grants, including funding opportunities, research and statistics, educational publications, and other items of interest. I found their "Forecast of Funding" particularly useful.

www.ed.gov/legislation/FedRegister/announcements/index.html
The Federal Register of the U.S. Department of Education. Provides application notices and other items of interest to educational-grant seekers.

www.findarticles.com
Research articles here to support your grant projects/programs.

www.firstgov.gov/Business/Nonprofit.shtml
Official information about and services for nonprofits from the U.S. government. A rich treasure of government resources and information can be found on USA.gov.

www.foundationcenter.org
The Foundation Center's Web site has a wealth of information for grant seekers. It provides a thorough course on proposal writing in its online library and is an excellent starting point for locating foundation/corporate funding sources.

www.fundsnetservices.com
Information about funding sources and grant writing, with many links.

www.givingforum.org
This Web site for the Forum of Regional Associations of Grantmakers provides numerous links to regional associations.

www.govspot.com
Links to state agencies and a wealth of government information. An exceptionally helpful Web site.

www.gpoaccess.gov/fr/index.html
Federal Register, published by the Office of the Federal Register, National Archives and Records Administration (NARA). This is the official daily publication for rules, proposed rules, and notices of federal agencies and organizations, as well as executive orders and other presidential documents. Information regarding federal grant opportunities can be found here.

www.grantsalert.com
Provides assistance with locating funding for educational grants. Offers many excellent links and resources.

www.grants.gov
Managed by the U.S. Department of Health and Human Services, this is excellent place to find and apply for federal government grants. This

Web site is a central storehouse for information about more than 1,000 grant programs, providing access to approximately $400 billion in annual awards.

www.grantstation.com
Allows grant seekers to identify potential funding sources for their programs and/or projects.

www.guidestar.org
Maintains a database of foundation/corporate funding sources.

www.internet-prospector.org
Will help you research almost any topic related to grant proposals and funding.

www.lexis-nexis.com
A database that provides information on individuals throughout the United States. Helpful when searching for funders, especially wealthy individuals.

www.marquiswhoswho.com
Who's Who in America provides information about individuals in the United States and worldwide. A good resource for finding wealthy funders.

www.nptimes.com
The NonProfit Times Web site includes links to recent articles and special reports pertaining to nonprofits, including information about foundations.

www.nsf.gov
The National Science Foundation provides many educational funding opportunities.

www.philanthropy.com
The Chronicle of Philanthropy is a biweekly newspaper that covers the nonprofit world and is an important resource regarding all areas of the nonprofit sector. Their Web site includes many relevant articles about gifts and grants, fund-raising, managing nonprofit groups, and technology. It also provides information on job opportunities and upcoming conferences and seminars.

www.technograms.com
Links to government technology grants and grants for students/educational purposes.

www.techsoup.org
TechSoup provides a range of technology services for nonprofits, including news and articles, discussion forums, and discounted and donated technology products. The site has many excellent links.

www.thompson.com
Thompson Publishing Group offers listings of publications focusing on grant and funding issues. Press releases announce developments in corporate and foundation funding. Additional services, such as grant deadlines and links to Web sites, are available to subscribers.

Search Engines

www.google.com
Use Google to locate wealthy individuals (as well as other funding sources) and conduct project/program research.

www.yahoo.com
Another search engine to use in your funding search, for conducting project/program research, to find articles, etc.

Print Resources

There are also many excellent print resources available to grant writers. Visit the Foundation Center's Web site (www.foundationcenter.org) for a list of libraries across the United States that maintain a collection of the Foundation Center's print materials. Visit a nearby library and examine their collection of grant-writing resources. Most of them will be housed on the same shelf, or close together. You will not be allowed to check these resources out, since they are considered reference materials.

If your local library is not listed, do not worry. You will find some grant-writing materials in even the smallest library. Do not limit your funding search to just the Internet. You will find many potential funding sources in print materials. Once you spend a little time reviewing the resources at your library, you will see how to use them to locate potential funders. Remember one of the most important funding-search strategies: Look in your own backyard first. Locate funders in your own city and state before searching farther afield; then, if necessary, locate funders who contribute on a national basis.

Appendix C

Sample Federal Grant

THIS IS an excellent example of a federal pass-through grant proposal written by a large urban school district. As you will see, this grant required a great deal of time and thought. Federal grants can be more involved than other types of grants, but the rewards are worth the time and effort. Notice the use of tables and their effective use of color to present data.

Proposal Plan
Introduction and Results of Needs Assessment

The _____ School System is a high-needs district of _____ students bifurcated geographically by race and by academic achievement. The schools in the northern part of the county enroll primarily non-Hispanic white and Asian students (Table 1), and students from these high schools boast SAT scores well above the state and national averages. In contrast, the overwhelmingly African-American, and primarily low-income, schools in the southern portion of the county post cumulative SAT scores more than one hundred points below the already low state average. Other standard measures of school academic achievement, such as elementary school Competency Test and End-of-Course Test scores show the same distribution pattern (see Table 2 for third-grade science scores). In recent years, a third region in the middle of the county has developed, where the schools are fully integrated and academic achievement has a more complicated profile. Overall, 37 percent of students enrolled in _____ County schools are eligible for the Free and Reduced Lunch Program, making it officially a "high-need local education agency" eligible for the Math/Science Partnership Program. These students are overwhelmingly located in South _____ County. The academic weaknesses are not confined to the low-income schools in the southern part of the county. A closer look at the data reveals that students of color perform weakly across the county, even in schools that boast the high test scores typical of affluent suburban schools (see Table 1 for Algebra and Geometry scores and Table 2 for Biology and Physical Science scores). In an effort to decrease this racial achievement gap, and to improve performance overall, it is critically important that all teachers be highly qualified, both in terms of disciplinary as well as pedagogical content. In particular, teachers need to be well versed in their basic math and science content, and also in the types of problem-solving, research, and data-analysis skills that support active-inquiry learning. Teachers also need to be able to adapt the examples used in their classroom lessons to better contextualize the content to reflect the culture and interests of their particular students.

Table 1

Mathematics End-of-Course Test-Failure Rates
County 2005–06, by School and Region

School Name	All	Female	Male	White	Black	Hispanic	Low Income	ESOL	Disabil.
Algebra									
County	29	29	30	9	51	41	53	46	63
High schools in northern part of county									
	27	33	22	15	51	38	49	36	48
	31	33	30	19	44	46	44	62	62
	20	15	24	16	44	33	32	NA	62
	26	32	22	25	26	40	42	NA	44
	16	20	14	18	15	NA	17	17	51
	20	19	21	10	36	29	37	32	49
High schools in central part of county									
	42	36	48	27	45	54	52	68	64
	42	42	42	22	40	67	55	68	71
High schools in southern part of county									
	76	73	80	NA	76	NA	79	NA	95
	61	58	63	61	62	43	64	NA	92
	72	71	74	73	73	64	72	75	88
	71	66	75	NA	71	NA	76	NA	89

84

Table 1 (continued)...

School Name	All	Female	Male	White	Black	Hispanic	Low Income	ESOL	Disabil.
Geometry									
County	29	30	28	7	59	35	58	32	50
High schools in northern part of county									
	11	11	10	5	24	28	26	14	28
	14	14	14	9	27	28	31	38	52
	8	7	8	6	14	25	10	5	21
	10	11	9	9	28	0	NA	NA	55
	7	7	7	5	29	10	19	9	25
	13	13	13	8	26	30	27	47	25
High schools in central part of county									
	31	31	30	15	44	38	43	53	29
	25	25	25	5	50	57	50	33	NA
High schools in southern part of county									
	75	77	73	NA	76	NA	75	NA	88
	71	70	73	52	74	86	72	NA	94
	64	63	66	NA	68	46	66	55	93
	63	62	65	NA	63	NA	66	NA	NA
		=0	-25%		=26	-50%		=51	-100%

For large high-needs school systems such as _____, with substantial gaps in the level of academic performance between different demographic and socioeconomic groups, there are identifiable professional learning needs at all grade bands in both math and science. The previous Tech Math and Science Partnership program focused on middle school teachers and the roll-out of the new middle school math and science performance standards. The proposed program focused on the need to create a cohort of content-rich Mathematics and Science Teacher Leaders at the elementary and high school levels, clustered primarily in the low-income and high-minority schools of _____ County and the newly emerging middle region. The Commission's certification endorsements of mathematics and/or science programs for grades 3 through 5 was deemed to not be a feasible goal. Instead, _____, through this newly proposed math and science program (MSP). with the Science and Mathematics TLP, a cadre of designated Science and Mathematics Teacher Leaders who have demonstrated proficiency in math and/or science content, standards-based instructional strategies, data-driven instruction, and appropriate performance-based assessment techniques, and who have shown themselves to be highly effective teachers when judged on student academic performance measures.

Table 2

Science End-of-Course Test-Failure Rates
County 2005–06, by School and Region

School Name	All	Female	Male	White	Black	Hispanic	Low Income	ESOL	Disabil.
Biology									
County	37	36	37	11	59	64	65	78	73
High schools in northern part of county									
	16	16	16	7	36	29	44	41	60
	27	27	27	9	49	70	56	86	49
	15	12	17	10	31	44	39	45	42
	13	12	14	9	34	38	78	NA	66
	12	10	14	9	23	30	25	58	59
	27	26	27	10	51	70	70	84	63
High schools in central part of county									
	44	42	47	23	55	63	62	84	78
	36	40	32	13	50	85	73	90	94
High schools in southern part of county									
	75	75	75	NA	75	NA	76	NA	94
	68	64	72	62	70	59	72	NA	95
	67	64	70	64	66	79	67	100	96
	49	45	52	NA	49	NA	53	NA	75
Physical Science									
County	36	36	36	13	48	49	53	58	66
High schools in northern part of county									
	18	17	19	11	27	35	38	17	35
	19	15	23	12	20	39	32	57	70
	26	31	22	17	34	60	30	NA	55
	10	12	7	8	29	18	46	NA	30
	12	14	11	8	23	NA	15	50	47
	26	25	27	12	38	53	49	65	50
High schools in central part of county									
	33	34	33	22	33	70	39	68	68
	46	51	42	27	42	71	46	64	62
High schools in southern part of county									
	59	57	61	NA	60	NA	60	NA	92
	53	49	56	67	53	55	58	NA	94
	52	51	53	70	52	46	57	61	93
	51	47	55	NA	50	NA	57	NA	90
		=0-	25%		=26	-50%		=51	-100%

To help identify the pedagogical and content skills that grades 3 through 5 and 9 and 10 teachers in _____ County are least comfortable with, we administered a survey adapted from math and science teacher instruments designed by _____. The science and mathematics curriculum coordinators disseminated the Web link for the survey, created online using SurveyMonkey, and 275 teachers in grades 3 to 5 responded. Data was arranged into two groups: Not Adequately Prepared and Somewhat Prepared in one group, and Fairly Well Prepared or Very Well Prepared in the other. Table 3 shows the results of the Pedagogical Skills survey. The highest needs are highlighted in orange and the next highest in yellow.

Table 3

Elementary School Teacher Self-Assessment of Preparation in Pedagogical Skills
Survey administered December 2006. 275 respondents

Question: Please indicate how well prepared you currently feel to do each of the following in your math and science instruction.	Not Adequately Prepared or Somewhat Prepared
a. Take students' prior understanding into account when planning curriculum and instruction	16%
b. Develop students' conceptual understanding of science and math	25%
c. Provide deeper coverage of fewer science and math concepts	34%
d. Make connections between science, math, and other disciplines	28%
e. Lead a class of students using investigative strategies	29%
f. Manage a class of students engaged in hands-on, project-based work	15%
g. Have students work in cooperative learning groups	12%
h. Listen/ask questions as students work in order to gauge their understanding	7%
i. Use the textbook as a resource rather than as the primary instructional tool	18%
j. Teach groups that are heterogeneous in ability	13%
k. Teach students who have limited English proficiency	55%
l. Recognize and respond to students' cultural diversity	17%
m. Encourage students' interest in science and math	9%
n. Encourage participation of females in science and math	7%
o. Encourage participation of minorities in science and math	11%
p. Involve parents in the science and math education of their children	38%
q. Use calculators/computers for drill and practice	27%
r. Use calculators/computers for science and math learning games	28%
s. Use calculators/computers to collect and/or analyze data	36%
t. Use computers to demonstrate scientific and mathematical principles	43%
u. Use computers for laboratory simulations	59%
v. Use the Internet in science and math teaching for general reference	21%
w. Use the Internet in science and math teaching for data acquisition	33%
x. Use the Internet in science and math teaching for collaborative projects with classes/individuals in other schools	49%

The highest needs identified by this survey, after the teaching of ESOL students, are related to the use of technology in the classroom and in the teaching of science and mathematics in ways that promote deep, integrated learning of fewer, important concepts, and to do so by incorporating investigative methodologies. High school mathematics and science chairs identified the same deficiencies in their teachers and also identified weaknesses in teachers' ability to take students' prior understanding into account, to use hands-on/project-based work, to use the textbook strictly as a resource, and to promote cooperative group work (data not shown).

The science content skills that elementary school teachers did not feel well prepared to teach at their grade level are listed in Table 4, and the mathematics content skills are listed in Table 5. The program staff will take these results into account when planning the specific content focus for the professional development program. However, we will also administer more detailed content knowledge assessments to both elementary and high school teachers at the beginning of the program to better define exactly where the gaps exist in teacher knowledge (see "Proposed Work Plan"). High school math chairs identified most of the same needs, except they reported a lower need for functions (25%) and algebra (4%), and a higher need for probability (43%) and data collection and analysis (36%).

Table 4

Elementary School Teacher Self-Assessment of Preparation in Science Skills (showing topics that at least 40% of teachers did not feel well prepared to teach)
Administered December 2006. 275 respondents

Question: Within science, many teachers feel better qualified to teach some topics than others. How well qualified do you feel to teach each of the following topics at the grade level(s) you teach, whether or not they are currently included in your curriculum?	Not Adequately Prepared or Somewhat Prepared
Modern physics (e.g. special relativity)	78%
Genetics and evolution	70%
Chemistry in general	69%
Structure of matter and chemical bonding	67%
Physics in general	67%
Chemical reactions	57%
Energy and chemical change	53%
Experimental design	45%
Electricity and magnetism	44%

Biology in general	42%
Forces and motion	43%
Energy	42%
Plant biology	41%
Structure and function of human systems	40%
Pollution acid rain global warming	40%
Environmental and resource issues in general	40%

Table 5

Elementary School Teacher Self-Assessment of Preparation in Math Skills (showing topics that at least 35% of teachers did not feel well prepared to teach
Administered December 2006. 275 respondents

Question: Within mathematics, many teachers feel better qualified to teach some topics than others. How well qualified do you feel to teach each of the following topics at the grade level(s) you teach, whether or not they are currently included in your curriculum?	Not Adequately or Somewhat Adequately Prepared
Calculus	87%
Mathematical structures (e.g. vector spaces, groups, rings, fields)	79%
Topics from discrete mathematics	78%
Functions (including trigonometric functions) and pre-calculus concepts	69%
Statistics (e.g. hypothesis tests, curve fitting, and regression)	67%
Algebra	39%
Technology (calculators/computers) in support of mathematics	36%

The other means of identifying specific content needs will be by analyzing the scores of standardized tests, disassociated by domain. Tables 6 and 7 show the scores on the 2006 math and science exams for grades 3 through 5, separated by different content domains. In our proposed Teacher Leader Program (TLP), teachers will conduct an in-depth item analysis of the scores of the students in their classes and school to identify the specific weaknesses and needs of the students. The results of these analyses, as well as the results of teacher content knowledge assessments, will help define the specific content knowledge that each particular teacher will explore during the summer institute.

Table 6

Spring 2006

	3rd Grade	4th Grade	5th Grade
Number Sense and Numeration	78%	81%	78%
Geometry and Measurement	74%	74%	73%
Patterns and Relationships/Algebra	69%	79%	78%
Statistics and Probability	86%	90%	73%
Computation and Estimation	81%	79%	77%
Problem Solving	71%	76%	72%

Table 7

Spring 2006

	3rd Grade	4th Grade	5th Grade
Inquiry	72%	72%	68%
Physical Science	63%	68%	61%
Life Science	76%	64%	65%
Earth Science	58%	61%	59%

Problem- and Project-Based Learning

One instructional strategy gaining prominence around the country for its effectiveness in promoting both deep mastery of content and an understanding in students of how to construct their own knowledge is problem-based learning (PBL). There are many variations on this pedagogical technique, and different practitioners refer to it as "project-based learning," "investigative case-based learning," or "challenge-based learning." PBL as an instructional tool addresses many of the pedagogical weaknesses identified by teachers. It promotes deep, integrated learning of fewer important concepts and incorporates multiple investigative methodologies, including the use of technology in teaching. _____ is at the forefront of implementing problem-based learning, with the introductory biomedical engineering courses and, soon, the systems physiology courses taught in this manner.

Proposed Work Plan

Goals and Objectives

<u>Program Goals</u>

Goal #1—To increase student academic performance in science and mathematics, particularly in the historically low-achieving schools in south _____ County.

Goal #2—To increase the number of Science Teacher Leaders and Mathematics Teacher Leaders in the elementary and high schools by enhancing 3rd–5th grade and 9th–10th grade teachers' skills in the following:

- Science and mathematics disciplinary and pedagogical content knowledge
- Data analysis and data-driven instruction
- Knowledge of standards-based instructional strategies
- Action research
- The ability to effectively assess student learning and sample student work

Goal #3—To increase teachers' and schools' use of student achievement data to inform and direct classroom instruction.

Goal #4—To increase teachers' and schools' use of standards-focused and project-based pedagogical strategies in the classroom.

Goal #5—To increase teachers' and schools' effective use of sample student work to benchmark the essentials of what students should know and do.

Goal #6—To involve building-level administrators in the mathematics and science professional development of their teachers, and to build support among administrators for the use of Standards-Focused Project-Based Learning.

Goal #7—To increase the number of faculty and students who actively participate in the _____ County Schools _____ partnership.

Specific Objectives

The specific objectives that support the aforementioned goals are:

Objective #1—Plan and implement the 2-year, 100-hour-per-year professional development program described below for 40 teachers in grades 3 through 5 and 40 teachers in grades 9 and 10 (20 mathematics teachers and 20 science teachers). Teachers will be chosen preferentially from the elementary and high schools with the lowest-performing students, as well as from other schools, by instructional math coaches and science and mathematics central office staff who have observed specific needs in specific classrooms. Preference will also be given to teachers from generally high-achieving schools who are involved in school initiatives to increase the math and science performance of their minority, low-income, and/or limited English proficiency students. Teachers will be encouraged to apply with other teachers from their school to help facilitate the implementation of school-based data-driven action research projects and standards-focused problem-based learning units, and to promote retention. Teacher compensation (financial and PLUs) will be awarded in a way that encourages retention in the program.

Measurable Outcomes:

1. 80 teachers will enroll in the program, with at least 70% of the teachers coming from schools in South _____ County and _____.

2. 75% of teachers will be part of school-level teams.

3. 90% of teachers will be retained in the program for the full two years.

Objective #2—Teachers will demonstrate increased mastery of science and/or mathematics content (where appropriate) between the beginning of Year 1 (fall 2007) and the mid-point of the program (fall 2008), and from the midpoint to the end of the program (fall 2009). Teachers will be tested using the endorsed instruments (such as Learning Mathematics for Teaching [LMT] and MOSART where appropriate and required for the evaluation. In addition, specific content-based tests will be created using questions from end-of-course and graduation tests, SAT practice tests, TIMMS studies, and other available content-specific instruments. These tests will be used by the teachers for self-assessment and for evaluation of individual and cohort content knowledge weaknesses and learning (see "Project Action Plan").

Measurable Outcome:

All teachers will show a significant increase in content knowledge at each testing point over the two-year period, using both types of instruments.

Objective #3 — The county school system will implement a successful Science Teacher Leader and Mathematics TLP.

Measurable Outcomes:

1. School system personnel will create the necessary infrastructure, including the purchase of application materials and the dissemination of information, to implement the TLP.

2. More than 75% of teachers enrolled in the MSP TLP will successfully complete all requirements to become a county Mathematics or Science Teacher Leader at the end of the program.

3. By the end of Year 2, 30 additional teachers will successfully apply for, and receive, science and/or mathematics Teacher Leader status.

Objective #4 — Teachers will demonstrate mastery of the use of student-achievement data to inform instruction, and will implement one-classroom or school-wide change based on the data, monitoring the effectiveness of the change through the use of action research.

Measurable Outcomes:

1. All teachers will successfully access, manipulate, and evaluate the student-achievement data related to their students, and will submit plans for one change based on the data.

2. More than 90% of teachers will submit plans for an action research project to monitor classroom change effectiveness.

3. More than 80% of teachers will submit action research results documenting the results of classroom change.

4. 50% of teachers will redeliver a data-driven instruction workshop to other classroom teachers by the end of Year 2.

Objective #5 — Teachers will demonstrate mastery of problem-based learning (PBL) as a pedagogical tool and be able to successfully utilize it in their classroom.

Measurable Outcomes:

1. All teachers will successfully participate in the PBL units utilized during the program institutes as measured by successful completion of institute deliverables.

2. All teachers will produce one PBL unit per year that supports a specific data-defined need in their classroom.

3. More than 90% of teachers will implement at least one PBL unit during the 2008–09 school year, and document results.

4. 50% of teachers will redeliver PBL instruction to other classroom teachers by the end of Year 2.

Objective #6 — Teachers will demonstrate mastery in performance-based assessment strategies and in the ability to effectively and consistently evaluate sample student work.

Measurable Outcomes:

1. All teachers will successfully score samples of student work using a rubric provided by _____ County.

2. All teachers will submit plans to redesign the assessment plan for one student assignment.

3. More than 90% of teachers will implement change and document results.

4. More than 90% of teachers will submit samples of student work for use by the program teachers.

5. 50% of teachers will redeliver performance-based assessment instruction to other classroom teachers by the end of Year 2.

Objective #7 — School-level administrators (principals, assistant principals, department chairs) and curriculum support teachers will become involved with the Math and Science TLP professional-development goals and objectives, and with all school-level project-implementation and action research plans.

Measurable Outcomes:

1. All project-implementation plans will require sign-off by a building-level administrator.

2. More than 75% of teachers will be observed by an administrator from his or her school during the implementation presentations (see Project Action Plan).

3. All principals, curriculum support teachers, and curriculum assistant principals will receive updates on the program at their monthly meetings.

Objective #8—Faculty and students will become more involved with enhancing science and mathematics education in county schools.

Measurable Outcomes:

The partnership will grow, as determined by analyzing the social network connections and the County School System.

1. Professional-Development Program Details

Recruitment of Teachers

Science and mathematics teachers in grades 3 through 5 and 9 and 10 will be recruited initially through personal visitation based on the lowest achievement scores. Administrators will be contacted by the project coordinator and/or the directors of mathematics and science to identify the teachers who will most benefit from the support provided by this grant. The teachers will receive a stipend of $1,350 and ten professional learning units (PLUs) for their participation. They will also be designated Mathematics and/or Science Teacher Leaders. They will be recognized and utilized by the school system as such (as described below).

School Year 1—August '07–May '08
(40 hours of professional learning)

The Mathematics and Science TLP will commence with summer planning during the summer of 2007, leading to a series of six workshops to be held from August 2007 through May 2008. Both elementary and high school teachers will participate in these six workshops, grouped in teams by grade band and school. The emphasis during the school-year phase will be developing the data-analysis skills necessary to effectively use available student test data to inform classroom instruction (see below for SAMS training details), to promote active engagement by the teachers in their own professional learning through the use of detailed content knowledge assessments, and to engage teachers in action research and performance-based assessment. Teachers will design and implement classroom changes and action research projects based

95

on the needs identified through the student-achievement data and will discuss best-practices teaching and learning, exemplified by the work of Robert Marzano, Carol Ann Tomlinson, and others. Discussion of best practices will continue throughout the school-year days and during the summer institute.

Table 8

Professional Learning Sessions During '07–'08 School Year

#	Hours	When	Topic	Funding	Staff
1	6	Aug	Student Achievement Management System (SAMS) Training	Stipends	
2	6	Aug	Student Achievement Management System (SAMS) Training	Stipends	
3	8	Fall—release day	Teacher Content Self-Assessment, LMT/MOSART Assessment, Action Research Workshop	Substitute	
		(In school)	Teachers design Classroom Implementation and Action Research Plans		
4	6	Fall—Saturday	Present Action Research Plans, Assessment for Learning and Performance-Based Assessment Workshop	Stipends	
5	8	Spring—release day	Introduction to Standards-Focused Problem-Based Learning	Substitute	
		(In school)	Teachers develop "driving questions" that address their content weaknesses and classroom needs.		
6	6	Spring—Saturday	"Developing Mathematical Ideas" (DMI) Training, Diagnosing Science Misconceptions, Share "Driving Questions"	Stipends	

Two other major topics to be covered during the summer are an introduction to Problem-Based Learning and a workshop on how children develop science and mathematics concepts and misconceptions. The PBL workshop will be taught through the use of actual PBL modules, designed to address specific teacher content knowledge gaps identified during Day 3 (see Table 8). After this workshop, teachers will develop "driving questions" that address areas of student achievement weaknesses, as defined by student data. The development of student concepts will be covered as part of an introduction to the "Developing Mathematical Ideas" program (see below), and student misconceptions will be explored using resources such as "A Private Universe" materials from Annenberg Media.

Student Achievement Management System (SAMS) Training

The Student Achievement Management System (SAMS) was implemented by _____ in the fall of 2006 to administer and report the results of Checkpoints assessments at the beginning and end of the first
semester. By August 2007, teachers will have access to three years of historical data on _____, ITBS, EOCT, and SAT results. The system allows
teachers and administrators to manipulate the data at the local school
level. SAMS training provides teachers with access to the ALIGN module, where teachers can review and manipulate the Checkpoints data.
During the 2007–08 academic year, teachers will be able to use ALIGN
to access historical data about standardized tests and to review and manipulate data from their classroom and/or grade-level assessments.

Practice in interpreting data and designing interventions will be
emphasized in the MSP Teacher Leader training. Teachers will also ex-
tend their knowledge of ALIGN by learning how to create their own
reports. Teachers will also be trained on ASSESS, the module that will
allow teachers to create and link their classroom or grade-level assessments to standards and have them reported through ALIGN. During
Year 2, the SAMS "outreach" portal will also be introduced; this will
enable parents and students to access information. The outreach portal
also serves as the digital platform where teachers can post lesson plans,
assignments, events, etc., for parents and students.

Developing Mathematical Ideas (DMI) Training

DMI demonstrates children's thinking using print and video cases of
classroom episodes so that teachers recognize and value children as
mathematical thinkers. The DMI professional learning workshop trains
teachers to analyze children's thinking more effectively, increases their
understanding of how children's mathematical ideas develop and change
throughout the grade levels, promotes ways to support the development
of children's thinking, and helps teachers make better instructional decisions. It also deepens teachers' understanding of mathematics and helps
them develop an expanded sense of mathematics and what it means to
learn mathematics. The teachers in the MSP Teacher Leader program
will be given an introduction to this program, with encouragement to
participate in full DMI training through the school system.

Year 1 Summer: Problem-Based Learning Institutes (2008) (60 hours of professional learning)

During the 60-hour summer institutes, teachers will participate in standards-focused PBL exercises specifically designed to increase their content knowledge in topics identified as being weak on the initial teacher content knowledge assessments, and to strengthen their investigative skills. The elementary teachers will participate in one 2-week institute, and the high school teachers will participate in a separate 2-week institute, both held at _____. Details of the two institutes are described below. In each case, teachers will be assigned to teams based on their content knowledge needs and interests and will engage in PBL exercises led by PBL-trained facilitators from _____ and _____. Faculty and graduate students will be recruited to serve as content experts, based on the specific content needs and PBL modules being used. Because of the emphasis in this program on teacher self-assessment of content weaknesses, and of PBL in general with its central emphasis on self-constructed knowledge, these content experts cannot be specifically defined at this time. However, _____ has ample connections with both faculty and students at _____ and will be responsible for identifying appropriate experts to participate in the program on a daily or weekly basis.

Elementary Teacher PBL Institute

The elementary teacher PBL Institute will be planned and implemented in collaboration with _____. The elementary teachers will participate in LBD modules, conducting the actual PBL challenges and extending their knowledge even further through visits to related science and engineering labs and discussions with faculty and graduate students. LBD is a project-based inquiry approach to science, aimed originally at middle school students in grades 6 through 8, but here will be modified for teacher professional learning. The goal of LBD is for students, and now teachers, to learn science and math content deeply and at the same time develop the skills and understanding needed to undertake the solution of complex, ill-structured problems. The program accomplishes this by having students learn content in the context of trying to achieve design challenges. For example, to learn about forces and motion they design and build miniature vehicles and their propulsion systems, optimizing their performance until they can go over several hills and beyond. Rather than memorizing facts and formulas, students become involved in the scientific concepts being covered and learn them in service of completing the design challenges before them. As they work toward successfully achieving these design challenges, students get practice designing and running experiments, analyzing data and drawing conclusions, making informed decisions and justifying them with evidence, collaborating, and communicating. In our MSP Teacher Leader Program, teachers will participate directly in several LBD challenges, thereby deepening their content knowledge and their understanding of the integration of science and math skills, while experiencing firsthand the PBL method of learning. The teachers will also design their own PBL units based on the content needs of their students and that directly support the _____.

High School Teacher PBL Institute

Problems can also be developed around current events such as mad cow disease or decisions concerning life-support systems in compromised patients. All such PBL problems have the possibility of exposing students and teachers to the fast-paced nature of technological change and the requirement for innovative problem solving across disciplinary borders. More important, however, these kinds of problems require participants to engage in integrative thinking across disciplinary lines while emphasizing deep content and the inquiry skills that are integral to lifelong learning and that are stressed in the _____.

The high school math and science teachers will be grouped in cross-disciplinary teams consisting preferably of at least one teacher each from biology, physical science, and mathematics. The BME-focused problems require knowledge from all of these fields to develop an adequate solution, thereby breaking down the artificial barriers that high school teachers erect between the fields and emphasizing the practical applications of math and science knowledge. Problems that have been particularly effective in the introductory BME classes are ones that require investigation of the accuracy and intrinsic errors of biometric devices, such as digital thermometers, blood pressure meters, pedometers, heart monitors, etc. These investigations require a detailed understanding of the human physiology involved, the physical science and engineering utilized by the device itself, and the mathematics needed for data analysis and modeling. Several of these PBL problems have been included in the appendix. They, and other BME problems, will be adapted for use with the Teacher Leader Program to ensure that the teachers investigate content areas where they show specific gaps in their knowledge. Like the elementary teachers, the high school teachers will design at least one PBL unit each summer for implementation in their classroom, based on classroom student achievement weaknesses.

School Year 2: August 2008–May 2009 (30 hours of professional learning)

The Science and Mathematics TLP will require 30 hours of professional learning activities during the Year 2 school year. Teachers will meet four times to share PBL units and implementation plans, design and share action research projects to assess the success of changes in classroom practice, evaluate new classroom achievement data using SAMS, conduct further self assessments of content knowledge gaps, and plan redelivery of Teacher Leader topics to school colleagues. All teachers will be expected to plan, implement, and document redelivery of one of the topics covered during Year 1 of the Teacher Leader program. Based on individual school need, teachers may choose to redeliver SAMS instruction, PBL training, performance-based assessment, or the development of science and/or math concepts and misconceptions.

Year 2 Summer: Problem-Based Learning Institutes (2009) (60 hours of professional learning)

The Year 2 Summer Institute will be similar to Year 1, with the new PBL topics based on continued assessment of teacher content knowledge gaps and tailored to the individual teacher. PBL topics in Year 2 will also emphasize the use of technology to acquire and analyze data and to facilitate collaborative projects.

School Year Final Component (Fall 2009–Spring 2010) (10 hours)

After the second summer institute, teachers will meet twice during the following school year to share implementation plans, compare issues, and analyze action research findings and new SAMS data. During this school year, all teachers are expected to redeliver one topic to their colleagues, choosing from the same list as above.

County TLP

At the conclusion of the MSP Science and Math Teacher Leaders Program, teachers will be encouraged to apply for designation as an official County Science Teacher Leader or Mathematics Teacher Leader. Determination of Teacher Leader status will be assessed using a matrix that includes:

- Teacher qualifications and experience

- Knowledge of standards-based instructional strategies (measured by the number of standards-based professional development workshops recorded by the teacher)

- Ability of the teacher to evaluate a sample of student work using a scoring rubric

- Content knowledge measured by the originality of lesson plan strategies and pedagogical activities

- Measure of teacher's students' performance at benchmark and/or using standardized state tests

Teacher Leaders will be recognized at a County Board of Education meeting. They will be utilized in providing professional learning, designing and/or revising instructional units for district distribution, and in the writing of assessment items for our newly established item bank. Financial compensation over and above their regular salaries will be awarded for these services. In Year 2, Teacher Leaders will have their registration paid by the system to attend. Principals will be asked to sign an agreement to pay for travel and lodging from their cost centers.

Evaluation and Accountability Plan

The evaluation of this MSP Teacher Leaders proposal will be conducted by _____, with cooperative input and assistance from the school district. The district will collect registration and recruiting data, conduct observations, and cooperate to define what should be transferred from professional learning into classroom practice. _____ will also collect data, analyze data, develop and administer surveys, and create and analyze observation forms. The proposed evaluation plan is designed to provide objective feedback of both performance (formative) and results (summative) measures. The evaluation of the project emanates from the measurable objectives detailed earlier in the proposal using a Cluster Logic Model and will cover inputs, activities, outputs, outcomes, and impact.

Evaluation Questions:

1. Describe the program's professional learning pipeline: How many teachers has the program recruited, trained, supported via follow-up training, and retained?

2. What recruiting strategies, training, and support are offered to teachers?

3. How do participants react to training and support? (Guskey's Level One: Participant Reactions)

4. Has teacher content knowledge improved? (Guskey's Level Two: Participant Learning)

5. Are participating teachers using recommended pedagogical methods and teaching to the performance standards? (Guskey's Levels Two and Four: Participant Learning and Use of Knowledge and Skills)

6. What leadership and pedagogical support do teachers receive? (Guskey's Level Three: Organizational Support)

Methods: Each of the above questions will be measured as indicated in the tables below.

Question 1: Describe the program's professional learning pipeline: How many teachers has the program recruited, trained, supported via follow-up training, and retained?			
	Types of Data Collected	*Methods for Collecting Data*	*Analysis*
# of teachers recruited	Simple counts of participants	Registration database	Event and cumulative count
# of teachers trained			
# of teachers provided follow-up training			
# of teachers retained	Percentage retained	District personnel files	Annual percentage and cumulative count

Question 2: What recruiting strategies, training, and support are offered to teachers?			
	Types of Data Collected	*Methods for Collecting Data*	*Analysis*
Recruiting strategies	Criteria for selection	District and professional learning staff	Gap analysis comparing planned professional learning activities to activities actually provided
Training	Description of training activities		
Support	Description of support activities		

Question 3: How do participants react to training and support? (Guskey's Level One: Participant Reactions)			
	Types of Data Collected	*Methods for Collecting Data*	*Analysis*
Teacher satisfaction with training and follow-up support	Participant reactions after training and follow-up support	Paper and online feedback forms	Descriptive with qualitative analysis of open-ended responses

Question 4: Has teacher content knowledge improved? (Guskey's Level Two: Participant Learning)			
	Types of Data Collected	*Methods for Collecting Data*	*Analysis*
Pre/post content knowledge tests	LMT or MOSART	Paper-based	Sent to _____ for scanning and analysis

Question 5: Are participating teachers using recommended pedagogical methods and teaching to the Performance Standards? (Guskey's Levels Two and Four: Participant Learning and Use of Knowledge and Skills)

	Types of Data Collected	Methods for Collecting Data	Analysis
What pedagogical methods are teachers using?	Administrator observations	Paper-based	Qualitative and quantitative analysis of observation forms
Who participates in the professional learning communities?	Professional learning community meeting logs	Paper-based sign-in sheet	Descriptive statistics
What evidence of teaching and learning indicates that teachers are adopting the recommended pedagogical methods?	Teaching artifacts and student work rated against a checklist of what the program expects to see transferred from instruction into practice	Instructor checklist	Qualitative and quantitative analysis; gap analysis comparing planned professional learning activities to activities actually provided

Question 6: What leadership and pedagogical support do teachers receive? (Guskey's Level Three: Organizational Support)

	Types of Data Collected	Methods for Collecting Data	Analysis
Leadership and Pedagogical Support	Teacher survey	Paper or online	Descriptive with qualitative analysis of open-ended responses

Evaluation Activities, Responsibilities, and Time Frame:

Activities	Responsibilities	Time Frame
Collect registration information including those recruited, trained, supported, and retained	District	Start to 2 months
Description of recruiting criteria, training activities, and support activities	District or supporting professional learning provider	Start to 3 months
Event feedback forms		Throughout as events are delivered
Administer Pre/Post LMT/ MOSART	District	Annually (Pre: start to 3 months; Post: month 9 to month 12)
Observation forms development and analysis		Development: start to 2 months; Observations: throughout
Administrator observations	District and supporting professional learning provider	Throughout

103

Activities	Responsibilities	Time Frame
Professional learning community meeting logs	_____ creates; participants fill out	Throughout; data collected quarterly
Transfers checklist—list of what the professional learning providers expect to see transferred from instruction into practice	District, professional learning provider	Start to 3 months; revisited annually
Artifact and student work analysis	Professional learning provider	Annually from months 10 to 12
Teacher survey to determine leadership and pedagogical support	_____ develops, administers, analyzes, and reports	Annually from months 10 to 12

Reporting Schedule:

Evaluation data will be formally reported on a yearly basis with informal reporting occurring as data are collected and analyzed. Ongoing performance data (from the registration database, feedback forms, observations, surveys, and meeting logs) will be turned around to program staff as soon as it can be analyzed and communicated. Results measures (from the LMT, MOSART, and student work) will be reported to program staff once the data are analyzed and returned. An annual summative synthesis of the data will also be reported to program staff and used for accountability purposes.

Evaluation Use:

To ensure that the evaluation plan will provide useful, actionable information, the following programmatic changes may occur as evaluation findings surface. Evaluation findings may affect:

- Teacher recruitment strategies
- The design and delivery of professional learning
- The design and delivery of follow-up support from staff and leadership
- The sharing of best or promising practices among various districts supported by the Mathematics and Science Partnership Program. The evaluators are submitting proposals to support numerous MSP efforts. This allows for evaluative comparisons and sharing of best practices across districts.

Appendix D

Local Government Grant Application

THIS IS a good example of a local government grant application. Notice how the format differs from what we discussed in Chapter Four. Sometimes foundations, federal agencies, and state and local agencies have their own forms/format that you will need to complete/follow when seeking a grant. However, if the funding source does not require a specific format, use the one discussed in Chapter Four.

FACT SHEET

MISSION

_____, a grant-funded program sponsored by the _____ County Board of Commissioners, has been created to **expand and/or enhance** existing services of youth activity programs countywide that provide a variety of structured activities for children and youth. These community-based programs are ultimately aimed to improve the achievements, values, and attitudes of _____ County youth.

Each applying organization **must** provide one or both of the following in the form of an RFP:

Expanded Services: Increase the quantity by serving more youth and/ or opening out-services (i.e., enrollment, location, hours of operation, transportation) to become more accessible.

Enhanced Services: Improve the quality by adding to the services and/ or heightening the level of program services.

- Funding for programs will be aimed at direct services for children ages zero to eighteen. Priority will be given to organizations whose programming focuses on high-school age students, immigrant populations mentoring programs.

- Programs will be selected and must be located **within** _____ County Commission Districts.

- Funds will be restricted as follows:

- Capital expense; deficit reduction; projects that are not open to the public; and projects of a **religious nature that are designed to promote religious belief and/or practice and/or which have a basic, underlying religious theme or topic**.

- Funds may not be used to supplant previously committed funds.

ACKNOWLEDGMENT

If funded, all advertising, promotions, and other publicity in connection with the supported program(s) must include the following acknowledgment:

"Funding provided in part by the _____ County Board of Commissioners under the guidance of the _____ Program."

CRITERIA FOR FUNDING

The _____ program commits us to include a Community Advisory Board, appointed by the Board of Commissioners, in the planning and selection process. Additionally, a series of public hearings are held to elicit community input. This effort promotes community awareness, community ownership, and community empowerment.

ELIGIBILITY REQUIREMENTS

ALL items listed must be included in order for the application to be processed.

For returning agencies that have a current Basic Standards Certification, please submit one (1) copy of these exhibits:

1. Copy of current Basic Standards Certificate.

2. Recent (within two [2] years) audit conducted by a Certified Public Accountant. Audits must be for the fiscal year review period, ending between December 31 and December 31. This must be a full, signed, certified audit that includes an Independent Auditor's Report, expressing an opinion regarding all pertinent material aspects of the organization's finances. ("Independent" is defined as a third-party auditor, with a report on the auditing agency's letterhead.)

3. An original Certificate or Declaration of Insurance, issued to _____ County Human Services Department, for proof of insurance with a minimum of $1 million (aggregate) coverage and a "current" one (1)-year term.

4. Proof of two (2) other current funding sources (i.e., letters of commitment) and copies of award letters from other funding sources.

5. Where applicable, the organization must provide a use agreement to operate programs in facilities that are not managed by the applying organization.

For first-time applicants that do NOT have a current Basic Standards Certification, please submit one (1) copy of these exhibits:

Please note that all items must be included with the application, or the application will not be processed.

1. A letter from the Internal Revenue Service recognizing the organization as nonprofit and tax exempt under **Section 501(c)(3)** of the Internal Revenue Code.

2. A copy of the organization's **Certificate and Articles of Incorporation and Amendments** from the Secretary of State.

3. Recent (within two [2] years) audit conducted by a Certified Public Accountant. Audits must be for the fiscal year review period, ending between December 31 and December 31. This must be a full,

signed, certified audit that includes an Independent Auditor's Report, expressing an opinion regarding all pertinent material aspects of the organization's finances. ("Independent" is defined as a third-party auditor, with a report on the auditing agency's letterhead.)

4. An original **Certificate or Declaration of Insurance**, issued to _____ County Human Services Department, for proof of insurance with a minimum of $1 million (aggregate) coverage and a "current" one (1)-year term.

5. A copy of the most recent **Board Meeting Minutes** and a list of all **Active Board of Directors**, indicating who is the registered agent to sign contracts.

6. Provide proof of two (2) other current funding sources (i.e., letters of commitment) and copies of award letters from other funding sources.

7. Permits/license (as applicable to program operations).

8. Where applicable, the organization **must** provide a use agreement to operate programs in facilities that are not managed by the applying organization.

9. Submit documentation from the _____, recognizing the proposed _____ funded program as either a licensed program, a program exempted from licensure, or a program that does not need a license or an exemption.

CATEGORIES

Organization must offer services to children and/or youth that will meet one or more of the following needs:

Areas identified as program priorities during the _____ Town Hall meeting series are:

- Programs for teenage youth
- Programs for immigrant populations
- Programs for children with disabilities/special needs
- Mentoring programs

- Cultural – i.e., heritage and historical exploration

- Disability/Special Needs – i.e., special needs, physical and mental challenges, inclusion program

- Economic Development – i.e., vocational, employability, and entrepreneurial skills

- Educational Supportive Programming– i.e., school readiness, tutorial, academic exploration, and programs ultimately aimed to improve school performance

- Family – i.e., childcare, early childhood education, teen parenting, improving self-image, and counseling

- Health – i.e., nutrition, safety, health care and awareness, teen pregnancy prevention

- Social Development – i.e., social relationships, responsibility, and life skills (mentoring)

- Violence Prevention – i.e., drugs, rape, sexual harassment, bullying, guns, hate crimes, conflict resolution, and youth offender restitution programming

GENERAL INFORMATION

OPERATIONAL SPECIFICATIONS:

1. All programs must be accessible to all children regardless of their family's ability to pay.

2. The proposed project must take place in a facility that is accessible under ADA guidelines.

3. Programs will focus on, but not be limited to, after school, evenings, and/or weekends between June 1 and May 31.

4. Organization must be willing to display signage reflecting the words: "This is a _____ Site."

5. No "recreation" or "art-focused" agencies will be eligible for funding.

6. Each applying organization **must** provide one or both of the following:

    Expanded Services: Increase the quantity by serving more youth and/or opening out-services (i.e., enrollment, location, hours of operation, transportation) to become more accessible.

    Enhanced Services: Improve the quality by adding to the services and/or heightening the level of program services.

7. Applications must be completed on disk. All disks must be submitted with application.

APPLICANTS SHOULD SUBMIT THE **ORIGINAL** AND **FOUR HARD COPIES** OF THE PROPOSAL TO:

Address

City, State, Zip

(Human Services Department Staff and resources will not be used to make copies.)

The selection committee is composed of a Board of Commissioners.

THE DEADLINE FOR RECEIPT OF ALL COMPLETE APPLICATIONS IS FRIDAY, FEBRUARY 9, at 3:00 p.m.

INCOMPLETE APPLICATIONS WILL NOT BE PROCESSED.

PROGRAM INFORMATION

Please type or print in black or blue ink on all pages.

Enter the legal name of the organization (as it appears on the 501(c)(3) IRS Letter of the Amended Articles of Incorporation):

_____

In 50 words or less, describe your organization's purpose:

_____
_____
_____
_____

Web Address: _____
Mailing Address (ONLY if different)
Street Address: _____
_____
_____

City, State, Zip

Organization's District Location _____

Grant Contact Person: _____ Title: _____

Organization's Board of Director's Chairperson: _____

E-mail Address: _____

Phone #: _____ Fax #: _____

We certify that the information contained in this application is true and correct to the best of our knowledge and belief.

_____
Authorizing Official Signature - Board Chairman/President

_____
Name (print or type)

Telephone (Day) _____ Evening _____

_____
Second Authorizing Official - Executive Director,
General Manager, or Treasurer of the Board

_____
Name (print or type)

Telephone (Day) _____ Evening _____

PROGRAM INFORMATION

The following pages MUST be completed.

What is the official title of this program?

_____

In 50 words or less, summarize this program's goals:

_____

_____

_____

_____

What is (are) this program's location(s):

_____

District in which the program is located: _____

Program Start Date: _____ Program End Date: _____

# of Children Currently Serving: _____

# of Children During Grant Year: _____

Age Range of Children Served: _____

Type of Program (List the **ONE** most-fitting category) (i.e., Educational, Violence Prevention, etc. – see Categories, page 4): _____

Months of Program (Please check **ONE**):

❑ Summer   ❑ School Year   ❑ Year-Round

Days of Program (What days of the week?): _____

Hours of Program (Start time to finish time, for each day of the program):

Scope of Contractor's Duties Describe specifically what participants (children and paid staff) of the program will be doing with the County funds requested (Objective Format, please!):

_____

_____

_____

_____

PROGRAM SERVICES

Please respond to only ONE of the three following asterisks (*) per proposed program.

*If your organization is **EXPANDING** your program,

❑ How many children does your organization presently serve? _____

❑ How many children will your organization serve as a result of the proposed program funding? _____

Comment (if needed): _____

_____

*If your organization is **ENHANCING** your program:

❑ What types of programs does your organization presently provide?

_____

❑ What types of programs will your organization provide as a result of the proposed program funding? _____

_____

Comment (if needed): _____

_____

*If neither question appropriately applies, please describe how your existing program proposes to expand and/or enhance its services to children and youth. Be sure to describe the following:

❑ What are the present services, and how many children and youth are impacted?

_____

❑ What are the proposed expansions or enhancements of those services?

_____

_____

_____

_____

Amount requested: _____

Amount of request to support salaries and fringe benefits: _____

Amount of request to support operating expenses: _____

QUESTIONS

- What are the applicant's fees, and how will the applicant make the program accessible to all children regardless of their family's ability to pay and regardless of the child's physical and mental abilities? (Attach a sliding fee scale, if applicable.)

- How will the applicant promote the program(s) or project(s)?

- How will the applicant evaluate the program(s) or project(s)?

- Describe the role of the applicant's board of directors/trustees and their overall effectiveness in achieving their goals and objectives.

- Does the proposed program require transportation? If yes, explain how the applicant will address that need.

- How does your agency accommodate children with special needs (i.e., type of activity or program modification)?

- Please provide any additional information about the applicant's program(s) or project(s) that is not covered elsewhere in this application, but that you believe is appropriate and relevant to the evaluation of the application.

- If you CURRENTLY receive _____ COUNTY FUNDS in the form of a _____ HUMAN SERVICES or _____ GRANT, please attach a sheet that reflects the type of grant, amount of the grant, and the scope of services that are provided with the specified funds.

PROJECTED BUDGET for Proposed Project/Program

All entries on this form should concern ONLY the project(s) that is (are) to be expanded and/or enhanced.

Use the following categories as given. All expenses must occur between the start and end dates of the project/program. If your application is for more than one project, this form should be completed for each proposed project/program. Attach the required number of pages to show the budget for each project for which support is requested. **Attach a breakdown of all In-Kind Expenses and all Cash Expenses that exceed $1,000.00.** *Your application will be considered incomplete without a budget explanation page.*

Expenses	Cash A.	In-Kind B.
1. Personnel - Administrative		
2. Personnel - Direct Service Staff		
3. Personnel - Support Staff		
4. Outside Fees		
5. Outside Fees/Services - Other		
6. Space Rental		
7. Travel		
8. Marketing		
9. Catalogues		
10. Remaining Operating Expenses - Equipment		
11. Remaining Operating Expenses - Supplies		
12. Remaining Operating Expenses - Utilities		
13. Remaining Operating Expenses - Other		
14. Capital Expenditures		
15. TOTAL CASH EXPENSES (Add lines 1–14 A.)		(Cash column)
16. TOTAL IN-KIND EXPENSES (Add lines 1–14 B.)	(In-Kind column)	
17. TOTAL COST OF PROJECT (Add lines 15 + 16)		

PROJECTED BUDGET for Proposed Project/Program -continued-

(For existing project[s] **only**)	A.	B.
18. Revenue - Admissions		
19. Revenue - Contract Services		
20. Revenue - Other		
21. Support - Corporate		
22. Support - Foundation		
23. Support - Other Private		
24. Support - Federal		
25. Support - Regional/State		
26. Support - Local/County/City		
27. Applicant's Cash		
28. TOTAL CASH REVENUE (Add lines 18–27 A.)		(Cash column)
29. TOTAL IN-KIND REVENUE (Add lines 18–27 B.)	(In-Kind column)	
30. TOTAL INCOME OF PROJECT (CASH + IN-KIND)		
31. TOTAL AMOUNT REQUESTED IN FUNDS		

CHECKLIST—ALL items must be included in order for the application to be processed.

Please check all categories for which required exhibits are enclosed to verify that the application is complete. All copies must be in the order listed.

Please submit one (1) original and (4) copies of:
- All Application Sections: Profile, Projected Budget, Questions, and Assurances
- Assurances Form - Signed
- Application Diskette

For returning agencies that have a current Basic Standards Certification, please submit one (1) copy of these exhibits:

1. Copy of current Basic Standards Certificate

2. Recent (within two [2] years) audit conducted by a Certified Public Accountant. Audits must be for the fiscal year review period, ending between December 31 and December 31. This must be a full, signed, certified audit that includes an Independent Auditor's Report, expressing an opinion regarding all pertinent material aspects of the organization's finances. ("Independent" is defined as a third-party auditor, with a report on the auditing agency's letterhead.)

3. An original Certificate or Declaration of Insurance, issued to _____ County Human Services Department, for proof of insurance with a minimum of $1 million (aggregate) coverage and a "current" one (1)-year term.

4. Proof of two (2) other current funding sources (i.e., letters of commitment) and copies of award letters from other funding sources.

5. Where applicable, the organization must provide a use agreement to operate programs in facilities that are not managed by the applying organization.

For first-time applicants that do NOT have a current Basic Standards Certification, please submit one (1) copy of these exhibits. All items must be included with the application, or the application will not be processed.

1. A letter from the Internal Revenue Service recognizing the organization as nonprofit and tax exempt under Section 501(c)(3) of the Internal Revenue Code.

2. A copy of the organization's Certificate and Articles of Incorporation and Amendments from the Secretary of State.

3. A recent audit conducted by a Certified Public Accountant. This must be a full, signed, certified audit that includes an Independent Auditor's Report, expressing an opinion regarding all pertinent material aspects of the organization's finances. ("Independent" is defined as a third-party auditor, with a report on the auditing agency's letterhead.)

4. An original Certificate or Declaration of Insurance, issued to _____ County Human Services Department, for proof of insurance with a minimum of $1 million (aggregate) coverage and a "current" one (1)-year term.

5. A copy of the most recent Board Meeting Minutes and a list of all Active Board of Directors, indicating who is the registered agent to sign contracts.

6. Proof of two (2) other current funding sources (i.e., letters of commitment) and copies of award letters from other funding sources.

7. Permits/license (as applicable to program operations).

8. Where applicable, the organization must provide a use agreement to operate programs in facilities that are not managed by the applying organization.

9. Submit documentation from the _____, recognizing the proposed _____ funded program as either a licensed program, a program exempted from licensure, or a program that does not need a license or an exemption.

Note: New agencies who are awarded _____ funds will have until December 31 to successfully complete the County Basic Standards certification process.

Have you...

1. Answered all questions fully and completely?

2. Enclosed a sliding fee scale for your proposed project, if applicable?

3. Obtained all official signatures?

Incomplete applications will not be processed.

All completed applications are due on or before Friday, February 9, at 3:00 p.m.

ASSURANCES

This provision will be extended to cover all subcontracts. The applicant assures and certifies with respect to the Grant that:

1. It possesses legal authority to apply for the grant; that a resolution motion or similar action has been duly adopted or passed as an official act of the applicant's governing body, authorizing the filing of the application, including all understandings and assurances contained therein, and directing and authorizing the person identified as the official representative of the applicant to act in connection with the application and to provide such additional information as may be requested.

2. No person shall, on the basis of race, color, sexual orientation, gender, age, national origin, or disability, be excluded from participation in, be denied benefits from, or be subjected to discrimination under any program or activity for which the applicant receives _____ County financial assistance.

3. The following statement will be included by the applicant when implementing a project funded with _____ County funds: "No person shall, on the basis of race, national origin, religion, sexual orientation, gender, age, or disability, be excluded from employment under a contract funded in whole or in part with _____ County Funds."

4. It will prohibit employment discrimination where: (1) the primary purpose of a grant is to provide employment, or (2) discriminatory employment practices will result in unequal treatment of persons who are or should be benefiting from the grant-aided activity.

5. It will establish safeguards to prohibit employees from using their positions for a purpose that is, or gives the appearance of being, motivated by a desire of private gain for themselves or others, particularly those with whom they have family, business, or other ties.

---

6. It will give the grantor agency, through any authorized representative, the access to and the right to examine all records, books, papers, or documents related to the grant.

7. It will inform the grant's manager of any major change in the organization (i.e., new director, new location, new telephone numbers, etc.).

8. The State of _____ prohibits the use of public funds in any way that advances, either directly or indirectly, the purposes of any sectarian institution. The agency assures under penalty of law that the receipt of public funds from _____ County is not in furtherance of any sectarian institution.

_____
Authorizing Signature
President/Board Chairperson

_____ Calendar

Date	Action
August	Public notification of Town Hall meetings
September	Neighborhoods in Action
December	_____ Grant applications distributed
February	_____ application deadline, 3:00 p.m.
March	Advisory Boards receive applications for independent review.
March	Advisory Boards meet by district to collectively review eligible applications.
April	AB recommendations forwarded to _____ County Board of Commissioners.
April	_____ County Board of Commissioners Final Action. Approval letters sent to grant recipients.
April/May	Negotiation of Scopes/Contract Signature Process.
June	First half of grant award dispersed to school and year-round _____ Grantees, and full grant award dispersed to summer programs. _____ contact period is June 1st – May 31st.
September	Deadline for submission of end-of-year contract report and program performance report for _____ summer programs, ending August 31st.
September	Neighborhoods in Action
January	Deadline for submission of mid-year contract report for _____ year-round and school-year programs for the period June 1st – December 31st.
January	Deadline for submission of invoice for second-half payment for school and year-round programs. Balance of funds disbursed to _____ Grantees based upon final approval of the County Budget.
June	Deadline for submission of end-of-year contract report and program performance report for _____ school and year-round programs ending May 31st.

119

Appendix E

Sample Foundation Grant

THIS IS a small foundation grant written by a classroom teacher. The teacher did some things well in writing this proposal, while other things need improvement. Read through the proposal, and think about how you could improve this grant. Use the grant-writing rubric in Appendix F to evaluate this grant, then review my ratings at the end of Appendix F.

<School Letterhead>

Cover Letter

Dear Mr. _____,

    As an elementary educator, I have found research that suggests students at _____ Elementary School in _____ would benefit from assistance from the _____ Foundation, which is dedicated to supporting literacy efforts across America. I believe your foundation will be interested in assisting the development and growth of an after-school reading program for third, fourth, and fifth graders in need called Project R.E.S.C.U.E: **R**eading to **E**ngage **S**tudents' **C**uriosity, **U**nderstanding, and **E**xcellence.

    _____ Elementary School is a high-performing school; however, research of test scores and teacher input shows that there is a growing gap between students who are excelling and students who are in need of more focused reading intervention to become successful in their later years. Project R.E.S.C.U.E. is requesting financial support in the amount of $9,120.00. These funds will go directly to the reading instruction of students in the grades

---

3 through 5 at _____ Elementary, as well as the training and support necessary for their families, many of whom are ill-equipped to assist their children in the area of reading.

This program will be held at _____ Elementary and will be supervised by Mrs. _____ and her team, who have taught in public schools for a combined total of more than 65 years. The program is supported by our county-level literacy coach, our local literacy coach, and our school principal, Ms. _____. A complete proposal is attached for your review.

Thank you for your consideration. I believe you will see that our project is aligned with your mission of "supporting family literacy in the United States by fostering and promoting the development and expansion of new and existing literacy and educational programs" as we work to aid the families in need at _____ Elementary School.

Sincerely,

Project R.E.S.C.U.E.

**Reading to Engage Students' Curiosity,
Understanding, and Excellence**

Submitted by:

Name Goes Here

Third-Grade Teacher

_____ Elementary School

Address

Submitted to:

_____ Foundation

Table of Contents

Project R.E.S.C.U.E.
(**R**eading to **E**ngage **S**tudents' **C**uriosity,
Understanding, and **E**xcellence)

Abstract

John Steinbeck once said that "reading is the greatest single effort that the human mind undertakes, and one must do it as a child." Becoming a lifelong reader is certainly what we as educators wish for every student. Since reading is an essential component of every subject in every level of schooling, it is imperative that we as elementary educators provide our students with the very best tools possible. As reported in Reading at Risk: A Survey of Literary Reading in America, literary reading among all age groups in the United States is declining. The National Center for Education Statistics (2003) reports that more than two-thirds of United States adolescents, beginning in fourth grade, are struggling to read proficiently.

_____ Elementary School is a high-achieving school, three times earning the Platinum Award that represents the highest percentage of students meeting and exceeding standards. The 2006–2007 state test scores tell us that upwards of 90 percent of our third through fifth graders are meeting or exceeding standards on the state tests. This is wonderful news; however, there are students who are not meeting with success, or are meeting it on a minimum level. It is these students that our project will target. It is our belief that the 10 percent of students who are not meeting or exceeding standards are not getting what they need in the regular classroom during the regular school day. Project R.E.S.C.U.E. (Reading to Engage Students' Curiosity, Understanding, and Excellence) will give them the small-group and teacher attention that will help them to become successful readers and lifelong learners. It will also foster an open line of communication with their families, who often go unnoticed due to their relative lack of involvement as a result of their own level of education. These families want the best for their children; they are just unprepared to ensure literacy at the level that is needed for lifetime success. What these children really need is highly qualified, consistently master-level instruction delivered in a focused, small-group setting. Since most students here are excelling in reading, _____ Elementary does not have a plan for additional support in this area. This is why Project R.E.S.C.U.E. is needed.

Our goal with Project R.E.S.C.U.E. is to create an environment where students are actively engaged, given opportunities to process language, and taught to make connections, infer, synthesize, and ask questions. Students will use collaboration, readers' theater, one-on-one teacher-led pairs, and small, student-focused instructional groups. These sessions will occur after school hours and on school property. Each member of the Project R.E.S.C.U.E. team has proven to be a master teacher who uses the current best practices in the field of education. The program will run from mid-fall to mid-April and will meet twice a week for an hour each session. It is our goal to have five students per teacher. Our plan is to use school materials that are already available to us. We will be providing students important resources they need—time and our focused attention—but we need your help. We would like to request $9.120.00 to make this project happen for our students.

Project R.E.S.C.U.E. (**R**eading to **E**ngage **S**tudents' **C**uriosity, **U**nderstanding, and **E**xcellence) will keep many children from being burned by a life of poor reading skills. We at _____ Elementary hear the alarm bells and are ready to answer the call. Our students need the ladders of critical skills, questioning strategies, and comprehension skills that Project R.E.S.C.U.E. will provide. It is our honor to be part of the team of heroes for our struggling students. While the fires of illiteracy may burn brightly, your support, along with our project, will RESCUE each student from a lifetime of illiteracy. We need you to join us in being their heroes.

Background Information

_____ Elementary School has served the community since 1993 and is located in _____, in the city of _____, _____. Our area is settled in the western part of _____ County, which is the largest school system in the state. Our school is situated next to _____, which backs up to _____.

Our enrollment is currently 1,004 students. Our population is not diverse, as it includes 84 percent Caucasian, 10 percent African-American, 4 percent multiracial, and 2 percent Hispanic students. _____ Parent Teacher Association is very involved in the school and during the 2007–2008 school year served on more than 34 committees to support students and school functions. 100 percent of teachers belong to the P.T.A. and are committed to working together for the good of the students at _____.

Parents at _____ Elementary work hard to make sure their children attend school—the attendance was 97 percent in the 2007–2008 school year. In addition, last year's annual survey states that 95 percent of students and 97 percent of parents agreed that they felt safe and secure at _____ Elementary.

_____ Elementary School does not currently serve our students in any before-school or after-school programs. Historically, there has been a strong focus on the math and science areas for our high-achieving students. Some of the accomplishments highlighted in the 2007–2008 Accountability Report include the fifth-grade Future Problem Solving Team's competition in Colorado (one fifth grader placed third in individual competition); a class of Kindergarten students' winning entries to the state Student Media Festival, and a subsequent winner at the international level of competition; and five fifth-grade students receiving Presidential Fitness Awards. There were no highlights listed in the area of reading. Because the vast majority of our school is successful in reading, there are no current goals or plans for improved instruction. This lack of focus is hindering the development of the small subset of students that desperately need reading support before it is too late.

Needs Statement

The need for an after-school program for at-risk readers grades 3 through 5 is clearly evident from data collected by Project R.E.S.C.U.E. directors. Information gathered from local assessments, language arts progress reports, portfolio assessments, teacher surveys, and a review of current research has been used to develop this worthy program to "rescue" at-risk students and families and ensure their success as strong lifelong readers.

Our local assessments include a reading benchmark assessment that is given three times each school year. This benchmark assessment is meant to determine minimal standards. As shown in the chart below, there are students in each of our targeted grades who are not working up to the minimal standards. These students are in classes with 18 to 22 high-achieving students who are being challenged to advanced standards and who have a strong reading support base at home. The 37 students who are targeted for Project R.E.S.C.U.E. will benefit from longer segments of focused instruction at their individual level.

Grade:	Number of Students Not Meeting Minimal Standards by Class, 2007–2008
Third	1, 2, 1, 2, 1, 2, 1, 1 – totaling 11 students
Fourth	3, 2, 3, 1, 2, 2, 1 – totaling 14 students
Fifth	2, 2, 1, 3, 1, 1, 2 – totaling 12 students

To any one teacher, the number of students in his/her class who are not meeting standards is not an alarming number. As you can see, however, when all intermediate-level students totaled together are considered, the number is much more powerful.

_____ County Public Schools use a language arts report card that shows growth and progress in several areas of reading instruction. The chart below shows how many students are not yet achieving at the independent level in reading fluency and comprehension. It is the goal of each teacher for 100 percent of students to be reading at the independent level or higher by the end of the year.

Grade:	Number of Students Reading Below Independent Level, 2007–2008
Third	13
Fourth	15
Fifth	13

A reading portfolio is kept for each individual student each year. The contents of the portfolio include writing samples, diagnostic reading inventories, audiotapes of oral reading when warranted, and anecdotal notes from reading instructional groups in the classroom. Review of these portfolios suggests that students are not gaining the skills needed for them to read and comprehend grade-level materials independently.

As Project R.E.S.C.U.E. was being developed, teacher surveys showed that there were indeed several students in each class who were not achieving at the minimal level expected. Observation of teachers indicates that oftentimes the needs of the higher-achieving students were unknowingly met before those of the lower-achieving students. Some of the problems teachers identified include developmentally inappropriate activities for struggling learners, insufficient time devoted to small reading groups, and the inability to meet different learning styles.

Review of current research shows that the literacy needs of older students continue to grow each year. The article in Educational Leadership entitled "After Third Grade" states that reading performance among students in grades 4 through 12 has become a prominent topic. The author of this article, Gina Biancarosa, explains many strategies that are research-based and proven to bring success to these students. Included are direct, explicit comprehension instruction, self-directed learning, collaborative learning, strategic tutoring, and ongoing formative assessment.

128

Further research has also uncovered an alternative approach that consists of a more preventive model in identifying the kinds of support struggling students need. The model described in Educational Leadership's article "No More Waiting to Fail" explains the basic prevention steps that have proven effective for students who are struggling. These include steps to address the problem, selected instructional activities and assessments for students who have not achieved as expected, and weekly monitoring and data gathering to indicate progress.

The members of Project R.E.S.C.U.E. are dedicated to making this happen. The desire to help this small population of our community is strong. In a recent questionnaire, more than 60 percent of our highly trained instructional staff reported a willingness to be involved in the program. The families of our targeted students have also expressed an enthusiastic interest in becoming involved. In addition, the parents of students who are excelling in reading strongly support such a program. We need your financial assistance to make it happen.

Program Description

_____ Elementary School is a high-performing school; however, research of test scores and teacher input shows that there is a growing gap between students who are excelling and students who are in need of more reading intervention to become successful in their later years. Project R.E.S.C.U.E. (Reading to Engage Students' Curiosity, Understanding, and Excellence) is designed to bridge that gap. As outlined earlier in this proposal, Project R.E.S.C.U.E. will offer students at _____ Elementary School an opportunity to grow through the use of teacher-directed small groups, collaborative learning techniques, one-on-one instruction, frequent assessments to better plan future instruction, and timely strategy and skill lessons directly related to each student's need.

Project R.E.S.C.U.E. will benefit a group of approximately 37 to 41 third, fourth, and fifth graders at _____ Elementary School. The group will meet after the school day for one hour on two days each week for about 22 weeks from October through mid-April, concluding the program at about the time of our spring testing season.

_____ state standards test, the _____ will be one instrument that we use to evaluate Project R.E.S.C.U.E. We will be looking for students to score higher in the "meets" level of achievement than they have in the past. Another way that we will know our plan is successful is through the end-of-year classroom assessments that were mentioned earlier in this proposal. We expect students to meet or exceed the minimal standards on the local reading benchmark administered by the classroom teacher, and we expect students to perform in the "independent" range of the end-of-year progress report. In addition, instructors in our program will use a running record of reading by the student to best evaluate the child's reading ability, since it evaluates the actual process of reading for the individual child. This program will use components such as reading aloud, shared reading, guided reading, and independent reading to strengthen skills proven to enhance both reading fluency and comprehension.

Since reading instruction has a myriad of different looks in an elementary setting, it is imperative that each teacher understands their students' learning styles and established strategies. We are incorporating several sessions for teachers in the program to sit one-on-one with their students to effectively evaluate and plan the most successful route for each student. One of the most important parts of reading instruction in grades 3 through 5 shows students how to approach reading material to learn information. Our program will address additional skills such as features of a textbook, features of genre, vocabulary, and graphic sources. Since each student will be evaluated at the start of the program timeframe, we will also end our program with benchmark evaluations to gauge how much learning has taken place.

One innovative aspect of Project R.E.S.C.U.E. is that our groups will be flexible and not structured strictly by grade levels. It is important that our teachers collaborate extensively using the Professional Learning Communities model, because the students in the program will be taught by the team of instructors, not just the particular teacher to which the student is assigned. The block of classrooms used will be clustered together for easy management of the program and more effective teacher collaboration and coaching.

Since students will be attending Project R.E.S.C.U.E. after a full day of school, we feel that it would be beneficial for students to have a small snack to help transition their day from large-group learning to small, focused-learning groups and working in a different learning environment. We feel the snack time will give students both a chance to socialize with others, since peer collaborative efforts will come into play in our program, as well as fuel them for the new tasks ahead. We want the children to feel energized, ready to participate, and have a positive feeling of ownership in their own learning.

It is through these components that we believe success will occur. Our mission is to give each student and family the care and attention they need to tap into their own curiosity of learning and a new level of reading understanding to ensure an overall level of excellence.

Program Goal

Our goal is to create an environment where students are actively and individually taught the skills and processes of reading that they have not mastered. Attaining this goal is crucial to the students' and their families' long-term, lifelong need to reach their full potential as active and literate members of our school community and enjoy academic success.

Program Outcome

As a result of participation in Project R.E.S.C.U.E., students will become more confident, successful readers. This will be done in a setting where small groups, collaborative efforts, and frequent assessments are used. Increasing students' reading confidence and skill will show an increase in reading standardized test scores, which will result in an increase in reading success for each student. Families will learn new strategies to support their readers at home.

Program Objectives

Project R.E.S.C.U.E. seeks to support students through the following objectives:

- 100 percent of participating students will make gains on his/her reading post-test benchmark.
- Small-group instructors will be provided with collaboration time.
- Families will receive opportunities to come to school to learn how to reinforce reading instruction at home.

Evaluation

Project R.E.S.C.U.E. will be evaluated in both formative and summative forms. Through formative evaluation, we will ensure that evaluation is ongoing throughout the program and all students will benefit from instruction. Through summative evaluation, we will assess the program at its conclusion.

The following table represents our plan for formative evaluation. Each objective in the program has a stated activity (or activities) that support(s) that objective. In addition, each activity has a stated outcome, assessment, timeframe, and person responsible. There are three stated objectives for our goal to create an environment where students are actively and individually taught the skills and processes of reading that they have not mastered.

To evaluate our program in summative terms, post-test scores will be collected and compared to student's pre-test scores in order to show growth in the area of reading comprehension and fluency. These scores will show that students have become stronger readers as a result of being a part of this program. We will use the portfolios that teachers will keep of students' formative evaluations, as well as their observations, anecdotal records, and the minutes from teachers' collaborative planning sessions. In addition, we will use the end-of-project parent surveys to evaluate the support given to the community.

Formative Evaluation

Project Goal: To create an environment where students are actively and individually taught the skills and processes of reading that they have not mastered.

Objective #1: 100 percent of participating students will make gains on his/her reading post-test benchmark.

Activity	Outcome	Assessment	Budget	Timeframe	Responsible Person
#1 Flexible small-group setting for reading instruction	Increased reading standardized test scores	Post-test scores	$0.00	October–April Weekly Sessions	Project Director, small-group instructors
#2 One-on-one instruction with a highly qualified instructor	Increased reading standardized test scores	Post-test scores	$0.00	October–April Weekly Sessions	Project Director, small-group instructors

Objective #2: Small-group instructors will be provided with time to collaborate on student gains.

Activity	Outcome	Assessment	Budget	Timeframe	Responsible Person
#1 Teachers are provided with eight sessions to collaborate	Increased reading standardized test scores	Post-test Scores	$9,120.00	October– April	Project Director, small-group instructors

Objective #3: Families will receive opportunities to come to school to learn how to reinforce reading instruction at home.

Activity	Outcome	Assessment	Budget	Timeframe	Responsible Person
#1 Families will receive four invitations to come to the school to learn strategies to support reading at home	Families will learn new reading strategies to help their child at home	End-of-program survey	$0.00	November January March April	Project Director, small-group instructors

Program Budget

Line	Budget Item	Grant Funds Requested
A	Teacher Stipends	$7,920.00
B	Office Supplies	$200.00
C	Copies	$500.00
D	Snacks for Students and Family Meetings	$500.00
E	**Total Grant Funds Requested**	**$9,120.00**

A. Six teachers will be paid $30.00 an hour. They will teach for two hours a week for 22 weeks (44 x $30.00 = $1,320.00 per teacher; $1,320.00 x 6 = $7,920.00). See Objectives #1 and #2.

B. The program will need office supplies such as pencils, red marking pens, loose-leaf paper, and folders for portfolios. All reading materials are already owned by the school. See Objectives #1 and #2.

C. Teachers will receive copies of journal articles that relate to reading instruction as necessary, copies of running record forms for formative assessment, and pre- and post-test benchmarks for summative assessments. Parents will also receive copies of pertinent reading strategies at the family meetings. See Objectives #1, #2, and #3.

D. Students will receive a snack each afternoon before small groups begin. Parents will also receive a snack when they come to the family support meetings in November, January, March, and April. See Objective #3.

Program Activities and Timeline
Project R.E.S.C.U.E.

	October	November	December	January	February	March	April
Students/ Teachers: Student Evaluations (Pre-test, post-test)	Week 1	Week 4		Week 1		Week 1	Week 1
Students/ Teachers: Weekly Sessions	Mondays Thursdays	Mondays Thursdays	Mondays Thursdays	Mondays Thursdays	Mondays Thursdays	Mondays Thursdays	Mondays Thursdays
Students/ Teachers: Formative Assessments	Weekly	Weekly	Weekly	Weekly	Weekly	Weekly	Weekly
Community: Family Support Meetings		Week 4		Week 4		Week 4	Week 2
Program Teachers: Collaborative Meetings to Discuss Student Progress	Week 3 Week 4	Week 2	Week 1	Week 2	Week 2	Week 2	Week 1
Community: Parent Survey							Week 2
School: Staff Meeting to Discuss Program	Week 1						Week 4

Appendix

A. Resume of Program Director

B. Statement of Assurances

C. Letters of Endorsement

D. Parent/Family Survey (Summative Assessment)

FAMILY SURVEY

My child is currently in grade (check one):

❑ Three   ❑ Four   ❑ Five

How many family meetings did you attend?   ❑ 0   ❑ 1   ❑ 2   ❑ 3   ❑ 4

Did you feel that the meetings were beneficial in providing you with strategies to help your child in the area of reading? Please explain. _____

_____

_____

What are some additional ways our school can assist you next year? _____

_____

_____

What is one strategy that you will most likely use with your child? _____

_____

_____

Do you feel more comfortable discussing your child's reading ability with his/her teacher? _____

_____

E. Bibliography

Biancarosa, Gina (2005). "After Third Grade." *Educational Leadership*, (63)2, 16–21.

Brown-Chidsey, Rachel (2007). "No More Waiting to Fail." *Educational Leadership*, (65)2, 40–46.

National Center for Education Statistics (2003). "The Nation's Report Card: Reading 2002." National Endowment for the Arts (2004), "Reading at Risk: A Survey of Literary Reading in America."

Appendix F

Grant-Proposal Rubric

CATEGORY	4	3	2	1	Points
Cover Letter	Includes a concise overview of the proposal, not to exceed one-and-a-half pages.	Includes a concise overview of the proposal, not to exceed one-and-a-half pages.	Includes a concise overview of the proposal.	No cover letter.	
	Includes the purpose for approaching this funding agency.	Includes the purpose for approaching this funding agency.			
	Includes the amount requested.	Includes the amount requested.			
	Sent to the attention of a specific individual.	Sent to the attention of a specific individual.			
	Includes a brief description of your organization (background information).				
	Typed on official letterhead.				
	Includes a request to set up an appointment or meeting to further discuss the details of your proposal (if local).				

CATEGORY	4	3	2	1	Points
Title Page	Has a catchy project title. Includes the name of the school or school system. Includes the Project Director's name and position. Includes your address, phone number, and the date (and your Web site, if available).	Contains three of the desired elements.	Contains two of the desired elements.	No title page.	
Abstract	Gives the reviewer a good picture of the proposed project. Clear and concise. Catches the interest of the reader. Explains the purpose and outcomes of the project.	Explains the purpose and outcomes of the project.	Abstract present, but the project's purpose and outcomes are not clearly stated.	No abstract.	
Background	Provides background information about your school/ system. At least one relevant unique feature is mentioned. Appropriate demographic data is provided.	Provides background information about your school/ system. At least one relevant unique feature is mentioned. No demographic data is provided.	Background information is present but does not include a unique feature.	No background information.	

138

CATEGORY	4	3	2	1	Points
Needs Statement	Explains why the project, program, or service is needed, providing any and all pertinent documentation. Examples of relevant documents include: Needs assessment Statistical data Literature review Surveys Explains a direct relationship between the identified need(s) and the project. Includes expected benefits of the project and who will be served.	Explains why the project, program, or service is needed, providing any and all pertinent documentation. Examples of relevant documents include only one or two elements.	Explains why the project, program, or service is needed.	No needs statement.	
Program/ Project Description	Contains a narrative explanation of the program/project implementation and how the need will be addressed. Includes clearly written project/ program goal(s), objectives, activities, timeline, and evaluation procedures.	Contains a narrative explanation of the program/project implementation and how the need will be addressed. Includes at least three clearly written elements.	Contains a narrative explanation of the program/project implementation and how the need will be addressed. Several elements are missing and/ or not clearly written.	No program/ project description.	
Project/ Program Goals	Clearly stated and attainable. The goal(s) strongly supports/reflects the need.	Most are clearly stated and attainable. Goal(s) supports/ reflects the need (could be stronger connection between goals and need).	Not clearly stated, and most are not attainable. Goal(s) do not support/reflect the need.	No project/ program goals.	

CATEGORY	4	3	2	1	Points
Objectives	Realistic, specific, and measurable. Concise: No more than 8 to 10 objectives. Congruent with stated need. Support the goal(s). Can be evaluated.	Realistic, specific and measurable. Concise: No more than 8 to 10 objectives. Congruent with stated need. Support the goal(s).	Not realistic, specific, or measurable. Not congruent with stated need. Do not support the goal(s).	No objectives.	
Activities	Procedures/ activities are tied directly to objectives and are carefully explained to the reader. A timeline for implementation has been established for each activity.	Procedures/ activities are tied directly to the objectives and are carefully explained to the reader. No timeline.	Procedures/ activities are not tied directly to the objectives.	No activities.	
Project Timeline	Supplies a projected timeline for the project/program, detailing the key stages of project preparation, implementation, and evaluation.	Supplies a projected timeline for the project/ program with limited detail of the key stages of the project.	Limited detailing of the project/ program stages.	No project timeline.	
Project/ Program Evaluation	Includes a clear introductory narrative detailing evaluation procedures. Both formative and summative in nature. A clear program/ project evaluation design is evident. Activities are evaluated.	Includes a clear introductory narrative detailing evaluation procedures. Both formative and summative in nature.	Only summative or formative evaluation is provided.	No program/ project evaluation.	

CATEGORY	4	3	2	1	Points
Budget	Figures are accurate and realistic. Directly related to the project's objectives and activities. Includes line items such as: Travel expenses Personnel Consultants Equipment Supplies Facility Includes a well-developed budget narrative.	Includes a projected budget. Figures are not accurate and/or realistic. Not directly related to the project's objectives and activities. Includes appropriate line items such as: Personnel Benefits Travel expenses Equipment Supplies Consulting Facility Other expenses Includes a budget narrative.	Includes a limited budget. Figures are not accurate and/or realistic. Not directly related to the project's objectives and/or activities. Line items are missing. No budget narrative is included or it is inadequate.	No projected budget.	
Appendix	Includes at least four items that support the project/proposal, such as: Project Director's resume Statement of assurances Letters of endorsement Charts/graphs Literature review article Copy of survey All items are self-explanatory and able to stand alone.	Only three elements are included. All items are not self-explanatory and cannot stand alone.	Only two elements are included. All items are not self-explanatory and cannot stand alone.	No appendix.	

Sample Foundation Grant Ratings

(See Appendix E for sample grant.)

	Rating	Comments
Cover Letter	4	Good job.
Title Page	4	Contains all the elements. I liked the project title. Include your school's Web site (if you have one).
Table of Contents	4	Contains the appropriate elements.
Abstract/Executive Summary	4	Good overall. I liked the last paragraph.
Background	4	Appropriate background information.
Needs Statement	4	Again, a nice job overall. Good use of local data. Note: Use tables, charts, and graphs to present data when possible.
Program/Project Description	4	Always begin this section with a narrative explanation of your project/program (how it will be implemented and how you will address the identified need). Include innovative aspects of your project/program (i.e., flexible grouping in Project R.E.S.C.U.E.).
Program/Project Goal(s)	4	The goal is clear and attainable. Supports the identified need.
Objectives	2	Not all objectives are not stated in measurable terms. Develop specific and measurable objectives; this will greatly aid your evaluation component.
Activities	3.5	A timeline for activities was included. Be sure to explain activities in sufficient detail.
Project Timeline	3	Timeline software would have assisted in the appearance/look of the timeline.
Project/Program Evaluation	3	You must clearly state how the goal(s), objectives, and activities of a project/program will be evaluated (using both formative and summative evaluation). Not all objectives were stated in measurable terms. Activities were evaluated.
Budget	3.5	A straightforward budget. Budget narrative was present.
Appendix	2	Did not include the Project Director's résumé or any letters of support. The family survey was included.

Note: In order to have a strong grant proposal, you will want most (if not all) of your ratings to be in category four.

Index

CPSIA information can be obtained at www.ICGtesting.com
Printed in the USA
LVOW041922050213

318771LV00002B/346/P